PEACE
Living Free From Worry

NANCY DUFRESNE

Peace: Living Free From Worry
ISBN: 978-0-940763-38-8
Copyright © 2013, 2022, 2024 by Dufresne Ministries

Published by:
Dufresne Ministries Publications
P.O. Box 1010
Murrieta, CA 92564
www.dufresneministries.org

1-5000 2-3000 3-7500

Unless otherwise indicated, all Scriptural quotations are from the *King James Version* of the Bible.

Scripture quotations marked AMPC are taken from the *Amplified® Bible, Classic Edition (AMPC)*, Copyright © 1954, 1958, 1962, 1964, 1965, 1987 by The Lockman Foundation. Used by permission. www.Lockman.org

Printed in the United States of America. All rights reserved under International Copyright Law. Contents and/or cover may not be reproduced in whole or in part in any form without the express consent of the publisher.

Cover design: Nancy Dufresne & Grant Dufresne

Nancy Dufresne's photo © Dufresne Ministries

WORLD HARVEST
BIBLE TRAINING CENTER
MURRIETA · CALIFORNIA

TRAINING BELIEVERS TO MOVE WITH THE WORD & THE SPIRIT

FOR MORE INFO OR TO SUBMIT AN APPLICATION ONLINE, GO TO

WWW.WHBTC.ORG

OR CONTACT OUR OFFICE AT (951) 696-9258, EXT. 202

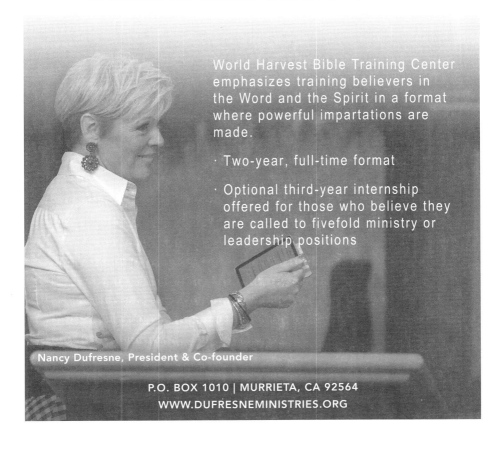

World Harvest Bible Training Center emphasizes training believers in the Word and the Spirit in a format where powerful impartations are made.

- Two-year, full-time format
- Optional third-year internship offered for those who believe they are called to fivefold ministry or leadership positions

Nancy Dufresne, President & Co-founder

P.O. BOX 1010 | MURRIETA, CA 92564
WWW.DUFRESNEMINISTRIES.ORG

Books by Nancy Dufresne

Daily Healing Bread From God's Table

His Presence Shall Be My Dwelling Place

The Healer Divine

Victory in the Name

*There Came a Sound From Heaven:
The Life Story of Dr. Ed Dufresne*

Visitations From God

Responding to the Holy Spirit

God: The Revealer of Secrets

A Supernatural Prayer Life

Causes

I Have a Supply

*Fit for the Master's Use:
A Handbook for Raising Godly Children*

A Sound, Disciplined Mind

Knowing Your Measure of Faith

The Greatness of God's Power

Following the Holy Spirit

*An Apostle of the Anointing:
A Biography of Dr. Ed Dufresne*

Victory Over Grief & Sorrow

Answer It!

The Price of the Double Portion Anointing

Worship

Love: The Great Quest

Books in Spanish

Pan Diario de Sanidad de la Mesa de Dios
(Spanish edition of *Daily Healing Bread*)

Contents

Introduction ix

1. The Sin of Worry 13
2. 4 Steps To Casting Your Cares on the Lord 39
3. Learn To Be Untroubled 63
4. What's Your Attention On? 73
5. Answer It! 97
6. Agree With God 99
7. Righteousness, Peace & Joy: A Divine Order 103

Prayer of Salvation 109

How To Be Filled With the Holy Spirit 111

Prayer To Receive the Holy Spirit 115

Introduction

Right thinking comes from the Word of God. When we feed on and receive God's Word into our minds and hearts, letting His words govern our thought lives, our words, and our daily actions, our lives will be transformed. The more we think right, thinking in line with the Word of God, the sweeter life will be.

Feeding and acting on God's Word runs out wrong thinking. Wrong thinking opens the door to the devil and closes the door to God. That's why Satan works continually to try to interject wrong thinking into our thought lives. Wrong thinking makes life hard, but right thinking opens the door to God and closes the door to the devil.

God can only work through right thinking. He is hindered from working for us the way He wants to when we think wrong. God is a perfect gentleman – He won't work uninvited. He's not like the devil, who tries to drive and force people. Right thinking invites God to work and move on our behalf.

Every thought that comes **to** you did not come **from** you. You are the custodian and steward of your mind and thought life; it is under your control. You are to learn to recognize wrong thoughts, reject them, and cast them down, refusing to turn them over in your mind.

Romans 12:2 instructs us, *"...be not conformed to this world: but BE YE TRANSFORMED BY THE RENEWING OF YOUR MIND...."*

One of the greatest needs of every believer is to renew their mind with the Word of God, for *a renewed mind is our greatest defense against the devil*. It keeps the door closed to him.

A renewed mind is a mind that thinks in line with God's Word; it's a mind that takes on God's way of thinking.

When a believer thinks and acts in line with God's Word, the devil has no place of entrance – the door is closed to him.

It is the life-long profession of every believer to further renew their mind with the Word of God; it's a joyous work we are to continue to do for the rest of our lives. As my spiritual father stated, "Your mind doesn't stay renewed any more than your hair stays combed." Just as our hair gets out of place, and we daily put it back, the mind will try to get out of place, and we must daily put it back and hold it in place as we continue to renew our mind by feeding and acting on God's Word.

As we feed and meditate on God's Word (building it into our spirit by thinking deeply into it and speaking and muttering it to ourselves) and act on that Word, our minds become renewed. Our minds aren't being renewed until that Word is being acted on in our everyday life.

A worried mind is an unrenewed mind. A troubled, worried, fearful, or depressed mind calls for further renewing with the Word of God. This is what will *transform* a life.

It takes effort on our part to renew our minds with God's Word. We must give time and attention to feed on God's Word and to prayer. But if that work is neglected, difficulties are experienced that could have been bypassed.

The devil can't work through right thinking; he can only work through wrong thinking. So he tries to interject thoughts that trouble you. You're going to hear the threats and suggestions of the enemy. You can't stop the devil from talking to you, but you can certainly have something to say when he speaks – answer him with what God's Word says. That's what puts him on the run!

Victory is not about getting the devil to leave you alone, because he won't. Victory is learning to quit listening to him and quit being troubled or disturbed by what he says. Don't believe or act on anything he says. Every believer can exercise their own authority over the devil and walk free.

If you're being mentally harassed, it's right and it's scriptural to have someone else pray for you, but you can also just take a stand against the enemy yourself and experience victory. You have the authority to resist the devil and tell him to leave. Answer those wrong thoughts with God's Word and hold fast to what God says, refusing to believe and entertain the thoughts of the enemy. Then praise God (in faith) that He has made you free.

All Christians need to further renew their mind and learn to act on the Word for themselves; that's how you close the door to the devil and keep it closed. That's how to experience lasting help; that's how you develop and mature spiritually.

You don't have to live a life of mental torment. You can live a life of total peace. You can live a life of Heaven on the earth. How? By renewing your mind with God's Word and taking on His way of thinking – changing wrong thinking to right thinking. You can live a transformed life!

Chapter 1

The Sin of Worry

Peace I leave with you, my peace I give unto you....

— John 14:27

The same peace that governed Jesus while He was on the earth, He left to us as part of our inheritance. It belongs to us. He made it ours.

Every person longs for peace. No one can count on this world or the circumstances of life to bring peace, for its source is divine. Jesus is the Prince of Peace (Isa. 9:6).

During His earthly life and ministry, Jesus was opposed and challenged by much opposition, but He lived completely untroubled and undisturbed, for those things were no match for the mighty force of peace that governed Him. And that same peace, He gave to us.

That peace comes into our spirits when we are born again. We don't have to ask Him to give it to us, for He's already made it ours, but we have to learn how to draw on and yield to that peace within so that we live the life of peace God authored for us.

We are the stewards and custodians of that peace Jesus gave us. Not only are we to draw on and yield to that peace, but we are to guard and protect it from things that will try to challenge and rob us of peace.

Don't Lose Your Peace

One of the primary ways that a believer loses their peace is by worrying. It's so easy to slip into worry and not realize it. It's something that we must guard against.

How do you know if you're worrying? If you're thinking about it!

Worry comes from fear and doubt. Fear and doubt are tormenting twins – they run together. When fear and doubt get together, they have a foul offspring called worry.

Many believers are living lives of worry and don't even realize it because they have lived that way so long that it has become normal to them. But that's not the life God authored for His children. God authored a life of peace and joy.

To yield to worry is to yield to fear and doubt, for if we weren't fearful of wrong things happening, we wouldn't worry. If we weren't doubting that God would fulfill His Word to us, we wouldn't worry. When anyone worries, they are yielding to fear and doubt as well.

Worry opens the door to depression and oppression.

Those who live depressed and oppressed have yielded to worry. To live free from that depression or oppression, they will have to stop worrying.

Some people are also troubled with anxiety and panic attacks. These things come from the spirit of fear, and it's a spirit we have total authority over. If fear tries to trouble you, speak to it and tell it to go in Jesus' Name!

Worry Breaks Down the Mind

The mind is not built to conduct worry, so if someone persists in worrying, their mind and body will eventually break down.

If you put diesel fuel in a gasoline engine, it will destroy the engine. It will break down and quit running because it's not built to conduct diesel fuel.

Likewise, God did not create the mind and the body with the ability to conduct worry, because worry isn't from Him. Worry will break down the mind and the body. Medical science has proven that to be true.

I once saw a report where a doctor stated, "Eighty-five percent of all disease begins from the shoulders up." In other words, eight-five percent of all disease comes because people allowed the wrong things to persist in their minds, which then affected their bodies. So, medical science shows that worry won't only affect the mind, but it will also affect the way the body functions.

Let's look at Matthew 6:25. Jesus said, *"Therefore I say unto you, Take no thought for your life...."* He's telling us not to worry about our lives.

The Amplified Classic Bible reads, *"Therefore I tell you, STOP being perpetually uneasy (anxious and worried) about your life...."* Just to be uneasy or anxious about something is wrong. That's worry! Many don't recognize it as worry, but it is.

Now, Jesus wouldn't tell us to stop worrying if we couldn't stop – that would be unjust – and He is not unjust. We can choose to stop being worried.

In that same verse, Jesus stated, *"Therefore I tell you, stop being perpetually uneasy (anxious and worried) about your life, what you shall eat or what you shall drink; or about your body, what you shall put on..."* (AMPC).

Jesus is telling us not to worry about what we eat, what we drink, or what clothing we have to put on our bodies. These are things we need every day. These are the *least* of the things that our lives require every day. If Jesus is telling us not to worry about the *least* of the things that we need every day, then He doesn't want us worrying about greater needs that we may have. Don't worry about *anything* that you may need, even down to what you eat, drink, or put on your body.

If He's telling us not to worry about what we are to eat or drink, then He certainly doesn't want us worrying about our mortgage, our jobs, our income, our families, or any other need.

Many don't even recognize that it's yielding to worry that has opened the door to mental harassment or depression.

But they can close that door by refusing to worry – refusing to turn those troubling thoughts over in their mind.

Worry Is a Sin

Since Jesus is telling us not to worry, then it's a sin to worry. If God says don't do something, then it's a sin to do it.

Matthew 6:27 reads, *"Which of you by taking thought can add one cubit unto his stature?"* Who has gotten taller from worrying about it? No one! No one ever went to bed worrying about their height and woke up to find themselves taller because they worried. Just as worry won't add height to you, worry won't add anything else to you!

No one went to bed worrying about their finances, their bodies, their children, or any other need, and woke up to find the situation resolved because they worried about it.

Go To Sleep in Faith

In fact, if you go to bed fearful or worried, you will leave the door open to the devil to attack you.

Psalm 127:2 reads, *"It is vain for you to rise up early, to take rest late, to eat the bread of [anxious] toil – for **HE GIVES [BLESSINGS] TO HIS BELOVED IN SLEEP**"* (AMPC). What are these blessings? If you'll go to bed trusting God, He will work on your behalf while you sleep. As long as you're in faith, trusting Him, then He can work for you.

But if you go to bed worrying, then He can't work for you, for worry isn't faith. God can't meet worry – He can only meet faith. You must have faith in God. It's your faith that gives Him permission to work on your behalf.

God is a perfect gentleman. He won't and can't do anything for you uninvited, and it's your faith that invites Him or gives Him permission to work on your behalf.

Now, demons and evil spirits will try to drive and dominate people, but God won't; He won't work uninvited.

Someone may say, "Well, God knows what I need, so if He wants to work on my behalf, He will." Yes, God knows what you need because He is all-knowing. But just because He's all-knowing doesn't mean He has your *permission* to meet that need.

I may know that you have a car, but just because I know that doesn't give me permission to drive it. You would have to give me your permission to drive it.

God knows what you need, but He can't work for you without your permission. Your faith is your permission. When you release your faith, you are giving God your agreement and your permission for Him to work.

How do you release your faith? Through the words you speak. For example, if you have a financial need, you can say, "Philippians 4:19 says, *'But my God shall supply all my need according to His riches in glory by Christ Jesus.'* Therefore, I believe that the supply God has for me is moving into my life now." That's how you give Him permission to supply the need that He knows you have; that's how you release your faith.

So, as you release your faith by speaking faith words, speaking God's Word, you leave the door open for Him to work and move in your life – even while you sleep. Go to sleep trusting God.

But if you go to bed worried and fearful, then you leave the door open to the devil, and he will work against you, even while you sleep. Refuse to go to sleep afraid. Deal with fear or worry before going to sleep.

Worry will not only open the door to the enemy, but it will destroy your faith.

Stand Against the Temptation To Worry

Worry is a sin because the Word tells us not to do it. If we're worried, we're in disobedience to His Word, and disobedience is sin.

Some treat worry like an option, but it's not; it's a sin, and you must treat it as a sin. Until you call it wrong, you won't take a stand against it and resist it.

If you were in need of money, and you saw money laying on the table at your friend's house, you wouldn't even entertain the thought of stealing that money from your friend because you know stealing is wrong; you would stand against that temptation to steal.

Likewise, worry is a sin. And when the temptation to worry comes to you, don't entertain it, but take a stand against it. Refuse to commit the sin of worry.

If you have been worrying, you need to recognize that it's a sin and repent of committing that sin. Purpose to stand against that temptation to worry just as you would against any other temptation to sin.

The Penalty of Worry

As we read in Matthew 6:25, Jesus instructed us not to worry because there's a penalty with it. The penalty is that it will close the door to God, open the door to the devil, break down the mind and body, and destroy our faith. Jesus doesn't want us to suffer the penalty that comes from worry, so He warns us not to do it. The penalty isn't from God – it's from disobedience.

When our children were younger, I would often warn them not to do certain things that I knew would hurt them because I didn't want them to suffer that hurt. If they would listen to me, they would be spared that hurt, but if they disobeyed, I could not keep them from being hurt.

We need to *listen* to God's Word. We need to call worry sin, and refuse to do it, and be spared the harm that comes from worry.

As previously stated, Matthew 6:25 reads, *"Therefore I tell you, STOP being perpetually uneasy (anxious and worried) about your life..."* (AMPC). When the Word tells us to *stop* doing something, we need to listen. He wouldn't tell us to stop if we couldn't stop; we can stop as we stand against the temptation to worry and as we think and speak in line with God's Word.

The Mind God Authored for Us

Second Timothy 1:7 tells us, *"For God hath not given us the SPIRIT OF FEAR; but of power, and of love, and of a SOUND MIND."* Fear is a spirit; it's not just a feeling – it's a spirit, and it's not from God. But it's a spirit we have authority over. When the spirit of fear comes, we are to speak to that spirit and tell it to leave us, and it must obey. For James 4:7 tells us, *"...Resist the devil, and he will flee from you."*

Second Timothy 1:7 also tells us that God has given us a "sound mind." I appreciate how the Amplified Classic Bible reads regarding a "sound mind." It says, *"...calm and well-balanced mind and discipline and self-control."* This is a picture of the mind God authored for us: a mind that is sound, calm, well-balanced, disciplined, and self-controlled. Don't settle for anything less than this, for this is what God authored for us.

Some have lived with worried, fearful, and troubled minds for so long that they don't even know what it's like to have a sound, calm, well-balanced, disciplined, and self-controlled mind.

God wants peace for you, but He must have your agreement and cooperation with His Word by you refusing to worry.

Stay in Peace

MARK 5:25-34
25 And a certain woman, which had an issue of blood twelve years,
26 And had suffered many things of many physicians, and had spent all that she had, and was nothing bettered, but rather grew worse,
27 When she had heard of Jesus, came in the press behind, and touched his garment.
28 For she said, If I may touch but his clothes, I shall be whole.
29 And straightway the fountain of her blood was dried up; and she felt in her body that she was healed of that plague.
30 And Jesus, immediately knowing in himself that virtue had gone out of him, turned him about in the press, and said, Who touched my clothes?
31 And his disciples said unto him, Thou seest the multitude thronging thee, and sayest thou, Who touched me?
32 And he looked round about to see her that had done this thing.
33 But the woman fearing and trembling, knowing what was done in her, came and fell down before him, and told him all the truth.
34 And he said unto her, Daughter, thy faith hath made thee whole; GO IN PEACE, AND BE WHOLE of thy plague.

Notice what verse 34 says, *"And he said unto her, Daughter, thy faith hath made thee whole; GO IN PEACE, AND BE WHOLE of thy plague."*

The Amplified Classic Bible reads, *"Go in (into) PEACE AND BE CONTINUALLY HEALED AND FREED from your [distressing bodily] disease."*

Because of her faith, she received the power of God into her body that healed her. But Jesus went on to tell her how to *maintain* the healing she had received, *"...Go in (into) peace and be continually healed and freed...."* If she was to maintain what she had received from God, she had to stay in peace.

What steals peace from you? Fear, doubt, and worry. Refuse to fear. Refuse to doubt. Refuse to worry. When you do, you will stay in peace.

The devil is busy trying to steal from you everything that God has ever blessed you with. As I stated previously, fear and worry open the door to the devil so that he can steal from you. But as you refuse to worry and fear, you stay in peace, and you keep the door closed to the devil.

If you lose your peace, you open the door to the devil – to sickness, lack, depression, and anything else he seeks to work against you. But if you stay out of worry and in peace, you keep the door closed to sickness, lack, depression, and anything else that comes from the devil.

Worry Closes the Door to God's Power

One of the reasons Jesus instructed us not to worry is because *worry closes the door to the power of God.* When we worry, the flow of God's power is interrupted in our lives. His power is hindered in our lives by worry. Worry closes the door to God's power, and then we can't receive the help we need.

If you are in your home with the door closed and a delivery man brings you a package, you can't receive that package until you open the door. If the door remains closed, you can't receive it, although it belongs to you.

Worry is the closed door that will keep that which God has for you from reaching you. God wants to help you, God has the ability to help you, but worry is the closed door that keeps His power out of your situation.

To receive the power of God that will change your situation, you must leave the door open to Him by refusing to worry.

Have you noticed that it's difficult to hear God when you're worried? He can't be easily heard through the closed door of worry. You can't hear anyone distinctly through a closed door. If a door is very thick and solid, it's difficult to hear at all. Worry puts a solid barrier between you and God, making it very difficult to hear Him.

God never abandons us, but worry is the closed door that keeps Him and His power from reaching us.

No wonder Jesus warned us not to worry. We need to have an unhindered flow of God's power into our lives, and worry hinders and interrupts that power.

Be in Position To Receive

Worry takes us out of position to receive what we need from God.

We've probably all found ourselves talking on our cell phones and then getting cut off because we lost the signal. There's an area in our home where our cell phones don't get a signal. If we happen to walk to that area while on our phones, we'll get cut off. So, we quickly *reposition* ourselves to a different area of the house so we can again get a signal. When we lose the phone signal, we can't conduct business any more on the phone until we get back in position to receive that signal.

Likewise, worry takes us out of position to receive from God. We can no longer conduct business with God when we're out of position to receive. We must reposition ourselves – we must get out of worry and back into faith. Faith never worries! *If we are worrying, we're not in faith. Faith receives from God – not worry.*

Break the Worry Habit

My spiritual father tells of the 16 months he was on his deathbed as a young man before he received healing from God.

He was raised in a home that was full of worry. He said that his mother and grandmother were "world-champion worriers." So, he learned the "worry habit" from them; he had worried his whole life.

At 16 years old, he became bedfast and was given up to die by medical science due to heart trouble and an incurable blood disease. The first day he became bedfast, he got born again. He received Jesus into his heart and was so thrilled to be saved. He had his mother bring him the Bible, and he began reading it, starting in the book of Matthew.

It wasn't long before he came to Matthew 6:25 and read that Jesus said, *"Therefore, I say unto you, Take no thought for your life...."* He realized that Jesus was saying not to worry. As he lay on his deathbed, that's all he had been doing – worrying about his body. Because he had such a habit of worry, he didn't know if he could stop worrying, so he tried to bypass that scripture. But as he tried to continue reading past Matthew 6, he wasn't getting anything out of it – the Bible seemed dark to him. When you don't do what the Word says, the Word will become dark to you. You have to be a *doer* of the Word if you want the Word to be light to you.

So, as a young man on his deathbed, he knew where he was missing God. God was dealing with him about that passage in Matthew 6, about the sin of worry. He was going to have to stop the sin of worry if he was going to receive what God had for him.

People know where they've missed it. People know where they're disobeying the Word. If they're to receive from God, they are going to have to be a doer of the Word.

If people stop walking in the light of the Word, stop doing what the Word says, the Word becomes dark to them, and they stop receiving from God. God wants to bless them, but they stop receiving from Him when they stop doing what He says in His Word.

That young man knew he was going to have to stop the sin of worry in his life. He was going to have to break the "worry habit." So, he repented of the sin of worry and committed to not worry again.

Now, at that time, as he lay on his deathbed, he was having anywhere from three to five heart attacks a day. Every time he would have one, he would hold on to the headboard to try to hold on to life and keep from dying. He had held on so much that he had worn the varnish off the headboard.

One day, when he had a heart attack, he again grabbed hold of the headboard, but it dawned on him that this was an action of worry – worrying that he would die – so he let go of the headboard because he had told God he wouldn't worry again. From that day on, he never had another heart attack.

Many are worrying without even realizing it. But as a young man, my spiritual father recognized that action of holding onto the headboard was worry, not faith, so he stopped it.

You Can Be Healed

At the time God was dealing with him about the sin of worry, he didn't even know that divine healing was in the

Bible; he didn't even know he could be healed. So, God was expecting him to stop worrying before he even knew he could be healed.

Why did God deal with him about stopping the sin of worry before He taught him how to receive healing? Since worry closes the door to the power of God, he couldn't even receive God's healing power until he stopped worrying. Also, even if God had healed him and raised him up off his deathbed, if he had continued to worry, he would have opened the door to the devil and lost his healing.

No one can maintain healing they've received from God if they're going to continue to worry. Remember the passage I referred to in Mark 5 regarding the woman healed of the issue of blood? After she received healing power, Jesus told her, "Go in peace and be continually healed." He was telling her to stay in peace so she could stay healed. He was warning her that if she lost her peace through worry, fear, or doubt, she would lose her healing. Worry robs from us.

That's why God dealt with my spiritual father about getting rid of worry before He healed him. He didn't want him to lose his healing by worrying. Until he stopped worrying, he could not have even received healing power, because worry closes the door to the power of God.

Is the Door Open or Closed?

Here's an interesting side note that will help you understand this further. A pastor once asked my spiritual father, "When someone in my congregation has fallen into a coma, it seems that I've not been able to help them; they would die. Is there something I need to know about ministering to someone in a coma?"

My spiritual father answered, "Yes, you will need to know the last thing they said before they slipped into that coma. Did they speak words of faith or words of doubt and unbelief?

"If they spoke words of faith, they left the door open to God, and God can help them. If they spoke words of doubt and unbelief, then they closed the door to God, and no one can help them – not even God."

Likewise with worry. Worry closes the door to the power of God, and no one can receive what they need from Him until they stop worrying. But faith opens the door to the power of God, so stay in faith and refuse to worry, and receive His power.

If you recognize that you've been worrying, you can change now. Repent for worrying and decide to put your trust in God, refusing to worry.

When someone is in faith, they're in peace. Great faith, great peace. Little faith, little peace. Guard your peace and guard your faith. Refuse to worry, fear, or doubt.

Established in Peace

I've taught our congregation that if they need healing, finances, or anything else, before they start making confessions of healing or prosperity, to make sure they're established in peace and not in fear or worry. Confessions of the Word won't work when they're made from a place of worry or fear, but they will work when they're made from a place of peace, for faith and peace move together.

If you're in peace, you'll be in faith. If you're not in faith, you'll be in worry, fear, or doubt. So make sure you're established in peace before you start making confessions of healing, prosperity, etc., for then you know you're in faith, and faith is the place of receiving.

You establish yourself in peace by feeding and meditating on the Word and on peace scriptures and by refusing to worry, fear, or doubt.

From that place of peace, confess the Word regarding healing, prosperity, or any other need; then you'll get results.

A Vision of Jesus

My husband and I were joined by about ten other ministers on a trip to St. Petersburg, Russia. We were there doing a week-long crusade. There were several services a day, and these ministers preached some of the services with us.

One night, I was teaching on the sin of worry. After I taught, all the ministers joined us in exiting the auditorium while the pastor closed the service. As we were leaving the auditorium, a holy reverence fell over the congregation. We all sensed it. (When a holy reverence like that comes, it's usually because Jesus is present.)

After we made our way downstairs to the hospitality room, one of the ministers came to me weeping. He was weeping so heavily that it was several minutes before he could speak. Then he told me what had just happened to him. "As we were coming down the stairs, I saw Jesus there, and He was weeping. He said, 'Worry is the primary thing that keeps My people from receiving what I have provided for them.'"

That Jesus was weeping shows His longing to help His people. He wants to help them; He wants to work in their behalf, but worry closes the door to God. Where there is worry, there is the absence of faith. Without faith, God cannot move to bless His people.

A Lesson on Faith

In Matthew 9:29, Jesus said, *"...According to your faith be it unto you."* God can only move in our lives according to the measure of faith that we release. God only responds to faith – not worry, fear, or doubt, but the enemy responds to those things and works against us when we operate in worry, fear, or doubt. God works for us when we release our faith.

Someone may have faith, but it won't benefit them until they release it. How is faith released? Through words and actions. When words of faith are spoken, faith is released.

The faith in your heart is released through the words you speak and the actions you take. The faith in your heart can't get out until you speak the Word or act on the Word. Your faith can't be heard until you speak. It's not enough to *have* faith – you must *release* it to benefit from it.

Romans 10:10 shows us this. *"For with the heart man believeth unto righteousness; and WITH THE MOUTH confession is made unto salvation."* Faith must be in two places – in your heart and in your mouth.

Mark 11:23 also shows us this:

> **For verily I say unto you, That whosoever shall SAY unto this mountain, Be thou removed, and be thou cast into the sea; and shall not doubt in his heart, but shall believe that those things which he SAITH shall come to pass; he shall have whatsoever he SAITH.**

In this verse, Jesus instructed us three times to "say." As you speak your faith in God's Word, things will obey you. Talk to them! As you speak, your faith is released, and God's power meets faith.

Don't speak words of worry, fear, or doubt, but speak words of faith. Then God can work on your behalf.

Worry Isn't Faith

That Jesus was weeping when that minister saw Him makes an impression on me. It shows His longing to help His people, but worry keeps His longing from being satisfied; He can't help them. When His children worry, the door is closed to Him, because worry isn't faith. *That which you worry about, God can't help you with.*

Faith for Every Arena

Did you know that you can be in faith in one arena of your life and be in worry over another arena of your life? God can move in the arena where you have faith, but He won't be able to move in the arena you worry about.

One minister told of the time he was financially behind in his ministry. He thought that every department was behind, but when he reviewed the financial report, he saw that every department was in the black, except for one. Then God spoke to him and said, "Did you notice that the only department that is behind is the only department that you worry about?" The minister saw that him worrying about that one department was what was causing that department to suffer financially.

Exercise faith for every arena: spiritually, mentally, physically, and materially. Don't worry about any of those arenas. If you worry about your body, it will open the door to sickness. If you worry about your symptoms, they will only increase. If you worry about money, it will keep money from coming in. If you worry about your children or family, it will hinder God from working on their behalf.

No matter what the need, don't worry about it. Stay in peace and stay in faith, trusting in God's Word, and then God will be able to work on your behalf.

How do you know if you are worrying? If you are thinking about it!

Don't Slip Into Worry

You have to continually refresh yourself in these truths so you don't slip into worry. You can walk with God for many years and still slip into worry without realizing it.

There was a wonderful Bible teacher who had taught the truths of divine healing for over 35 years and was strong in faith. But during World War II, she spent much time praying for the Jews. After a while, she began having mental problems and had a mental breakdown. She finally had to be committed to a mental hospital. While she was there, God showed her where she had missed it. She was worrying about what was happening regarding the Jews, and she was praying for them from a place of worry, not from a place of faith, and it eventually broke down her mind.

Praying "worried prayers" doesn't work. When we pray, it must be from a place of faith – not worry.

When she saw where she had missed it, she repented of worrying, and it wasn't long before she was again normal and dismissed from the hospital.

She had great faith, but had slipped into worry, and the worry hurt her faith. When she quit worrying, her faith again grew strong and robust, and she was completely restored.

No matter how long we have been saved, or how much faith we may have, we must guard against the sin of worry.

Jesus Comes to the Hospital

My spiritual father tells of an incident that happened to him in his earlier days of ministry.

After preaching a service one night, he exited through a side door to go outside. When he did, he slipped and fell on the ice that had built up on the step and hurt his arm. The pastor he was preaching for drove him to the emergency room. While on the way to the hospital, the Spirit of God spoke to him and said, "Your arm isn't broken, it's dislocated. Don't worry about it, and I'll talk to you about it later."

When he got to the hospital, the doctors confirmed that it wasn't broken, but was dislocated. However, to reset it, they would have to put him to sleep, which they did. Then they kept him in the hospital for a few days to observe him and make sure there were no negative effects from the anesthesia.

A couple of days later, he was sitting up in his hospital bed reading his Bible when he heard footsteps walking down the hospital corridor toward his room. He assumed the nurse was coming, so he looked up as the door opened. When he looked up, he saw it wasn't the nurse. It was Jesus.

Jesus pulled up a chair to his bedside and sat down and talked to him for the next one and a half hours. During the course of His visit, He told my spiritual father that the reason he had the accident was because he had gotten out of the will of God and opened the door to the devil, and the devil had attacked him.

What I want you to see is this: he had missed God and opened the door to the devil. Remember what the Spirit of God said to him when he was riding to the hospital? He told him, "Don't worry, and I'll talk to you about it later." Notice, *even though he had missed God, God still didn't want him to worry!*

Now, when Jesus walked into the room and pulled a chair up beside his hospital bed and talked to him, the first thing He said to him was, "I spoke to you by My Spirit when you were in the car riding to the hospital and told you that your arm wasn't broken, but dislocated. The doctors confirmed that to be true. I also told you not to worry, and that I would talk to you about it later. You haven't worried about it, and I commend you for not worrying."

Notice that one of the first things Jesus said when He appeared to him was to commend him for not worrying. That stands out to me. That must have been important.

I believe that if he would have worried, then Jesus couldn't have appeared and spoken to him for an hour and a half, for worry closes the door to the power of God.

I believe God wants to speak to and help many of His people, but they have closed the door to Him through worry.

Don't Worry – Even If You Miss It!

Another important thing to see from this is that my spiritual father had missed God and gotten out of God's will.

Yet, even though he missed it, God still didn't want him to worry, for worry closes the door to God. If he had worried, I don't believe Jesus could have appeared to him and showed him where he missed it and could not have spent that time talking to him.

When we miss God, we need His help more than ever to get us back on track. But if we worry because of sins, failures, or mistakes we've made, then we close the door to God, and He can't help us when we need it most.

It's one thing to be facing difficulties because the enemy is opposing and attacking us, but it's another thing to be facing difficulties because of our own sins, failures, and mistakes. But even then, we must confess it, forgive ourselves, and exercise our faith so God can help us out of those difficulties. We can't worry about it, even when we miss God, or our faith won't work and God won't be able to help us like He wants to.

God wants to help us, even when we miss it, so He tells us not to worry – because if we do, we close the door to the power of God. It pleases God to undertake for us. It pleases God when we receive His power, so let's refuse to worry, and let's receive of His power.

Chapter 2

4 Steps To Casting Your Cares on the Lord

Philippians 4:6 reads, *"Do not fret or have any anxiety about ANYTHING…"* (AMPC). How clear God's Word is to us that we are not to worry – about anything! Even if we miss God or fail, we are not to worry. Worry is a sin, and it is wrong for any believer.

The kind of life God authored for us is to live days of Heaven on the earth. *"That your days may be multiplied, and the days of your children…as the DAYS OF HEAVEN UPON THE EARTH"* (Deut. 11:21). You can't live "days of heaven upon the earth" if you're worried, for Heaven has no worries.

Since we are not to worry, what are we to do when the cares, the concerns, and the tests and trials of life come?

First Peter 5:7 tells us, *"Casting the whole of your care [all your anxieties, all your worries, all your concerns, once and for all] on Him, for He cares for you…"* (AMPC). We are to cast our cares on Him; when we do, then He can take care of them. But if we don't cast our cares on Him, giving them to Him, then He won't be able to work on our behalf. As long as we're worrying, then we're holding the cares in our own hands and not putting them in His hands to work on them.

Leave It With God

When I was about eight years old, the neighbors asked me to go with them to the carnival that had come to town. My mother told me I could go and gave me some money.

When we got to the carnival, I wasn't interested in going on any of the rides. There was a booth, however, that I was interested in, and that was a jewelry booth. I didn't have much money, but I was able to buy a necklace. Because it was so cheap, the links of the necklace were very thin and small, but that didn't matter to me – I loved my necklace. Because the clasp on it was small and delicate, it was difficult for me to take the necklace off, so I just left it on. I slept and bathed with it on.

Because the links were so small, after a few weeks, the chain had knotted badly. I tried to get it unknotted myself, but my fingers were too clumsy for the delicate job.

Finally, I took it to Mother and asked her to fix it. She took out a straight pin and began working to loosen and unknot the links. After a few minutes of working on it, I saw that the last knot was nearly completely undone. I was excited to see it almost undone, and I was sure I could finish the job myself. So, I quickly took it out of Mother's hand, saying, "I can finish it, I can finish it!"

As I tried to undo the loosened knot, I started pulling at it and only managed to get it back in a knot again.

Mother held out her hand and said, "If you will leave it in my hands, I'll finish the job, but if you're going to take it back, I can't fix it." So I handed it back to her, and she finished the job, doing what I couldn't do.

It's the same with God. If we will cast our cares and troubles on Him, putting them in His hands, then He can take care of them. But as long as they're in our hands, He can't help us, although He wants to.

Once we put those cares in His hands, then we have to leave them there and not take them back. If we will leave them in His hands, then He will finish the job.

It's for Our Benefit

God tells us to cast our cares on Him because He wants to work on our behalf. He's our Father, and He wants us to trust Him to take care of us; it is His pleasure to work on our behalf.

Isn't it much better to let God work on your behalf than you trying to work on your own? He's so much more capable of taking care of you than you are.

It's for our own benefit that He wants to work for us; we're the ones who will benefit from His help.

If you're worrying, that's a sign that it's still in *your* hands and not His. You've got to put your cares in His hands and leave them there.

When something tries to worry or trouble you, you must make the decision to refuse to worry, but instead, tell God that you are putting the care in His hands and trusting Him to take care of it. Then refuse to think about it; let it go out of your thought life. Don't hold onto it in your thought life, but rather praise God that He is taking care of it since you put it in His hands.

If the devil tries to again bring that worry or concern to you, or if you're awakened in the night with those thoughts or worries trying to trouble you, just tell the devil you refuse to take those worries or concerns back, quiet your mind, and begin to praise God that He is working on your behalf. Refuse to leave peace – stay in faith.

4 Steps To Casting Your Cares on the Lord

In God's Word, He gives us very definite steps to take to cast our cares on Him instead of worrying. We find these four steps in Philippians:

PHILIPPIANS 4:6-8
6 Be careful for nothing; but in every thing by prayer and supplication with thanksgiving let your requests be made known unto God.
7 And the peace of God, which passeth all understanding, shall keep your hearts and minds through Christ Jesus.
8 Finally, brethren, whatsoever things are true, whatsoever things are honest, whatsoever things are just, whatsoever things are pure,

whatsoever things are lovely, whatsoever things are of good report; if there be any virtue, and if there be any praise, think on these things.

The Amplified Classic Bible of verse 6 reads, *"Do not fret or have any anxiety about ANYTHING…."* I'm so thankful for that word "anything." No matter what it is, don't fret or have ANY anxiety about ANYTHING!

The first thing this verse says is not to worry. That's listed before we're told to pray. We're going to have to stop worrying before we can ever pray in faith.

You have to refuse to worry, then your faith will work, and when you pray, you'll get results. But if you're going to worry, then your faith won't work, and without faith working, your prayers won't get results.

Step #1 – Pray

The first step we're to take when tempted to worry, fret, or be anxious about anything is found in verse 6. We're to refuse to worry, but instead, *"…in everything by PRAYER and supplication with thanksgiving let your requests be made known unto God."* When tempted to worry or fret, refuse to. Instead, pray.

"Pray" means to talk to God. Anytime you're praying, you're talking to God, and anytime you're talking to God, you're praying. So, instead of worrying, talk to God about it.

To pray is to do something spiritual and supernatural (above the natural). When tempted to worry, which is carnal or natural, do something supernatural instead – pray – talk to God.

The natural thing to do when tempted to be troubled or to worry, is to talk to people about it. But that's doing something natural. Instead, do something supernatural – talk to God. He is your help – talk to Him about it.

James 5:13 tells us, *"Is any among you afflicted* (going through a test or trial)? *let him pray...."* If you're going through a test or trial, pray – talk to God about it.

Isn't it interesting that the Word reminds us that when we're going through a test to talk to God about it? Why does the Word remind us to do that? Because the natural thing to do is to respond naturally, either by worrying or talking to other people. But instead, we're reminded to respond spiritually – do something supernatural – talk to God about it.

Again, Philippians 4:6 reads, *"...in every thing by prayer and SUPPLICATION...let your requests be made known unto God."*

Prayer, in its *general* sense, means to talk to God. But this verse says, *"...by prayer and SUPPLICATION...."* It's telling us a *specific* way to pray – with supplication.

"Supplication" is not a casual request, but an earnest, heartfelt request. It carries with it the idea of pouring out your heart to God. Supplication involves being very specific – pouring out *specifically* every detail of your heart.

When something tries to trouble you, God invites you to offer supplication – pray specifically – pour out every detail of your heart.

Too many times, people just think about, mull over, or mentally rehearse that which tries to trouble them instead of pouring their hearts out to God.

Then other times, some pour their heart out to other people about their situation and omit talking to God about it. But when you pour out the specifics of your heart to God and leave your cares with Him, trusting Him to work on your behalf, then you won't keep talking about it to others, for you know He's got it.

You may want to set a point in time when you talk to God about it and cast it on Him. Then if the enemy tries to again trouble you about it, you can refer back to the point in time when you cast it on the Lord, reminding the devil that God is taking care of it and that you refuse to take it back.

Find Scriptures That Promise You Your Answer

The prayer of supplication involves making *specific requests*. When we have a need, we are to find specific scriptures that promise us our answer, and those are the scriptures we are to use as we pray. That's the way to get results in prayer – bring specific scriptures to God that promise you your answer, and release your faith as you pray those scriptures. A successful prayer life is based on the Word, not on feelings or emotions, so pray the Word.

When you know what God has promised you in His Word, and you release your faith in His Word, then you will refuse to worry, for you are assured that God will make His promise good in your life. You're resting on Him; you're not troubled.

Step #2 – Thanksgiving

Philippians 4:6 reads, *"Be careful for nothing; but in every thing by prayer and supplication WITH THANKSGIVING let your requests be made known unto God."*

Once we pray and offer supplication, pouring our hearts to God, then we are to offer another kind of prayer – thanksgiving – which is the second step to casting our cares on the Lord. We are to thank Him that since we have cast our cares on Him, we know they are in His hands and He is working on them.

> **1 JOHN 5:14 & 15**
> **14 And this is the confidence that we have in him, that, if we ask anything according to his will, he heareth us:**
> **15 And if we know that he hear us, whatsoever we ask, we know that we have the petitions that we desired of him.**

This passage lets us know that we can be confident that if we ask anything that's in line with His will (His Word is His will), He hears us. He doesn't hear us because we feel like He heard us, but rather, He hears us when we ask in line with His Word, regardless of what we may or may not feel. When we find specific scriptures that promise us our answer, and we bring those before God and release our faith in them, that's how we pray "according to His will," and then we know He hears us.

Verse 15 tells us, *"...if we know that he hear us...we know that we have...."* When we pray in line with the Word, we know He hears us. And when we know He hears us, we know we *have*.

In verse 15, God is letting us know that His hearing us equals us having our request. He lets us know that when He hears us, He sends the answer. He authorizes us to believe that when He hears us, we can count the answer ours.

Because He sends the answer at the time we pray, we are to give Him thanksgiving. That shows our faith in Him, that we believe He sends the answer at the time we pray, even before that answer manifests.

At the time we pray, God hears us and answers us, but there can be a passage of time before that answer manifests or shows up in our life. Praising and giving of thanks is what we are to do until our answer manifests. As we give thanks and we praise God, we are releasing our faith, so it helps to hold us in the faith arena and out of the mental arena. Praising holds our attention on God and the answer, and off the need.

Faith is of the spirit arena, not of the mental arena; your faith isn't in your mind – it's in your spirit. And praising God is one way of releasing that faith out of your spirit.

The natural mind wants to figure everything out, but faith flows out of your spirit, not your mind. Your spirit, your heart, can believe things that your mind can't figure out. In fact, if you try to figure out how God is going to cause the answer to manifest in your life, your mind will talk you right out of faith, because your mind can't "figure out" how God can supply your need.

If you prayed in line with God's Word, He heard you. When He heard you, He sent the answer. Until that answer manifests, give Him thanks – that's faith! That's how you continue to release your faith.

Quiet the Mind

An important part of faith is learning to quiet the mind so that it doesn't reason against the Word and talk you out of your faith in God. Quiet the mind, don't try to figure everything out, and just give Him thanks. As you do, your answer will continue to move toward your life, and it will manifest.

Praise Brings the Anointing

Praise brings the anointing, and it's the anointing that destroys the yoke (Isa. 10:27).

As you praise, God's anointing breaks off those things that try to trouble you. As you praise, your faith is strengthened. As you praise, you hold yourself in the faith arena and out of the mental arena. As you praise, you are releasing the faith that's in your spirit. And as you praise, it helps hold your attention off your need and onto God and His Word, which is your answer.

You will never receive the help you need from God if your attention is on your need, your worries, and your problems. Your attention must be on God and what His Word promises you – then His power will flow.

What your attention is on is what will flow in your life. Praise helps you hold your attention on God and His Word, and off your need.

What To Do With Troubling Thoughts

Years ago, when I was going through a particular test, the enemy was bombarding my mind with troubling thoughts. (You need to realize that all thoughts that come to your mind don't originate in your mind. The devil will suggest thoughts to your mind that bombard it, and they can trouble you if you don't know how to resist them.) I was handling those thoughts wrong, so I was troubled by them.

I made the mistake of trying to "get rid" of those thoughts. But I later realized it's not my job to "get rid" of those thoughts, because no one can keep the devil from talking to them.

Rather, I should have *answered* those thoughts by saying, "That thought is a lie, it will *not* come to pass, and here's what the Word says...." I should have answered the thoughts with the Word of God, then turned my attention away from what the enemy suggested and threatened me with.

Although I did answer those thoughts with the Word, confessing what the Word said, I didn't turn my attention away from what the enemy suggested as I should have. I kept turning those troubling thoughts over in my mind, trying to "out-think" them and "get rid of them." After answering them with the Word of God, I should have taken my attention off them, ignored them, turned my back to them, and resumed my life as normal. That's what Jesus did in the wilderness of temptation when He told the devil, "Get thee behind Me," in Luke 4. (For more teaching on this subject, see my book, *A Sound, Disciplined Mind.*)

But because I only partially did what I should have done, the thoughts the enemy suggested and threatened me with troubled me, and I became entrenched in worry, and it seemed I couldn't get my mind to stop turning those thoughts over.

The Praise Cure

After several months of this, the Spirit quietly spoke to me, "Apply the praise cure." I knew what He was referring to because in Lilian B. Yeomans' book, *Healing from Heaven,* she has a chapter titled, "The Praise Cure," and I remembered what she taught.

The Spirit led me to emphasize praising God. Now, don't misunderstand me. We should study, pray, and make confessions. But the Spirit of God was prescribing my answer to me. I saw that I had been doing these other things, but I hadn't been praising as I should – I had gotten behind in praise. I needed to catch up on my praise.

You know you can get behind financially, but you can get caught back up. You can get behind in sleep, but you can get caught back up. Well, I had gotten behind in praise, and I needed to get caught back up. So the Spirit prescribed that I was to spend as much time as possible praising, so I did.

When I woke up, I started praising. As I drove my car, I praised. As I was in my home, I praised. If I was alone, I would do it aloud, but if I was around other people, I would do it quietly to myself.

During the first several days of doing that, there came great pressure against my mind from the enemy threatening that praise was not enough to get me past this difficulty – but it was! The enemy tried everything to get me to stop. He wanted to draw me out of the faith arena and back into the mental arena, trying to figure everything out, but I just kept at it. After about two days of praising God all throughout the day, I realized that the greater pressure had subsided.

At the end of one week of praising God almost continuously, something in my spirit clicked, and God spoke to me, "Now, tell that evil spirit that has been harassing your mind to desist in its maneuvers against you." I did, and it stopped. That troubling didn't just stop all at once, but there was immediately a great relief, and over the next few days, the momentum of those troubling thoughts had completely subsided.

By praising, I had moved out of the mental arena and back to the spirit arena, the faith arena.

Praise was the cure. After months of great struggle and difficulty, when I started praising, the victory came. As one minister stated, "When you pray, you lay hold of things. But when you praise, you win battles!"

There's nothing you can't praise your way out of, and there's nothing you can't praise your way into.

Paul and Silas had been beaten and thrown into prison. But at midnight (the darkest hour), they praised, and the prison doors were shaken open (Acts 16). They praised their way out.

When God's people were marching around the city of Jericho, on the seventh day, they shouted and the city walls fell (Josh. 6). They praised their way in.

Sometimes you need out of something, and sometimes you need into something. Praise will get you out, and praise will get you in. It's the praise cure!

People talk about all kinds of different cures. Some may work some benefit some of the time, but there is only one cure that will work on everything every time. It's the praise cure!

We see why Paul instructed in Philippians 4:6, *"Be careful for nothing (do not fret or have any anxiety about anything – AMPC); but in every thing by prayer* (talking to God) *and supplication* (pouring out your heart to God and making specific requests using specific scriptures) *WITH THANKSGIVING let your requests be made known unto God."* Thanksgiving plays a vital role in the life of faith and in receiving what you need from God.

Step #3 – Yield to Peace

Paul went on to tell us the end result of doing the above verse, *"And the peace of God, which passeth all understanding, shall keep your hearts and minds through Christ Jesus"* (Phil. 4:7). Peace will be the end result of doing steps one and two – talking to God and making specific requests, and giving thanks.

Before Jesus left this earth, He bequeathed His peace to His disciples. He said, *"Peace I leave with you, my peace I give unto you…"* (John 14:27). The same peace that governed Him while He was on the earth, He left to us as part of our inheritance. It belongs to us. He made it ours.

The third step to casting our cares on the Lord is to yield to and draw on that peace within that He has made ours. Jesus went on in that same verse to tell us how to yield to and stay in peace, *"…Let not your heart be troubled, neither let it be afraid."* The way to stay in peace is to refuse to be troubled by or afraid of what comes against you.

If you've not been living in peace, now you know how to get back into peace – stop allowing yourself to be troubled, and stop allowing yourself to be afraid.

Don't wait for all the circumstances of your life to be peaceful, but learn how to yield to the peace of God that's on the inside of you, in your spirit, right in the midst of difficult circumstances, by refusing to be troubled or afraid.

Peace doesn't mean the absence of difficulties, but it means you've quit allowing circumstances to trouble or worry you.

Don't wait for the devil to leave you alone or to quit talking to you – he won't! But answer those things by speaking God's Word, then turn your thoughts and attention away from what the devil suggests by refusing to turn those thoughts over in your mind.

If you've been in the worry habit, it may take some time to break that habit, but start today by refusing to worry, and it won't be long before life will be different for you; you'll be enjoying a life of peace.

An Example of Peace

When my husband was in his late 50s, he was diagnosed with cancer. It was in his lymph nodes, and the doctors let us know that it was a serious condition.

After we walked out of the doctor's office, I got in my car (I had driven in a separate vehicle from my husband). Before

I even turned on the car, I did exactly what Paul instructed in Philippians 4:6 & 7. I told God, "You know my mind could go many different directions. I know it, and the devil knows it, but I refuse to let it! I refuse to worry about it, and I refuse to even think about it! If I let my mind run off any wrong direction, I'll just dig myself into a hole. And if we're to receive any help from You, I'll have to dig myself back out of that hole of worried, wrong thinking, so I just refuse to go there. I refuse to worry!

"Father, Jesus took our infirmities and bore our sicknesses, so healing belongs to us. I believe we receive the healing needed. And I'm just praising You for it." Then I quieted my mind and began worshipping God. For the next several minutes, I sat in that car and worshipped God, holding my attention on Him and His Word, and refusing to let my mind touch on the problem.

Within about three minutes, I tangibly felt what seemed to be like a blanket come down over my head and shoulders and rest there. It was that peace that passes understanding. My mind was so calm, peaceful, and untroubled, and it seemed as though I couldn't have even conjured up a worry if I had tried.

Before this time, I had been using the daily needs of my life to practice living free from worry. That's how I knew what to do when we received that diagnosis.

You don't become skillful at doing the Word without practice. Use the small, daily needs of life to practice living free from worry. Then when greater needs arise, you'll be skillful at applying the Word and exercising your victory.

When I arrived back at the house, I was in total peace. My husband was already back at the house when I came in. He said, "I've already talked to God about it. I told God that I know He doesn't miss it, so I must have missed it somewhere and opened the door to the devil to attack me. He spoke to me and told me two places where I opened the door to the devil. I repented of those, and when I did, God said, 'Alright, that cancer will be all gone within 30 days.'"

On the 29th day, my husband went back to the doctor for his appointment and had all the tests run. The doctor came back into the room and said, "Somebody up there likes you, because it's all gone!"

During those 30 days, I hadn't worried one time. We both had great peace.

Now, my husband told me later that when the doctor gave him the diagnosis 30 days earlier, fear struck him in his toes and started moving up his legs; he felt that spirit of fear trying to gain entrance. But he just talked to it and said, "No, you don't! You get back down." And it left.

Jesus said, *"Behold, I give unto you power* (authority) *to tread on serpents and scorpions, and over all the power of the enemy: and nothing shall by any means hurt you"* (Luke 10:19).

James 4:7 reads, *"Submit yourselves therefore to God. RESIST THE DEVIL, AND HE WILL FLEE FROM YOU."*

You have authority over the spirit of fear. When you feel or sense fear trying to trouble your mind, resist it! Tell it "NO!" Stand your ground against it.

That's what my husband did when fear tried to come, and it left!

Because we obeyed the Word and refused to worry, even in the face of difficult circumstances, God's power could work on our behalf. Even though my husband had missed God, he still didn't worry. If we had become fearful and worried, we would have closed the door to God's power, and He wouldn't have been able to help us. But being a doer of the Word keeps the door open for God's power to work.

Perfect Peace

Isaiah 26:3 reads, *"Thou wilt keep him in perfect peace, whose mind is stayed on thee: because he trusteth in thee."*

I like this phrase "perfect peace." In Hebrew (the Old Testament was originally written in Hebrew), this phrase reads, "Thou wilt keep him in shalom, shalom...." Double peace. It's a perfect peace.

When I think of a perfect peace, or a peace that is perfect, I think of uninterrupted peace. Not a peace that's "here today and gone tomorrow." It's a continuous, ever-present peace.

Jesus lived and demonstrated that perfect peace. He had constant difficulties opposing and surrounding Him, but He was completely untroubled by any of them. He is our example of peace, and He left us that same peace to govern us; it's a perfect peace – it works perfectly every time as we yield to it, no matter what difficulties may be present. We can be peaceful right in the midst of troubling circumstances.

Isaiah 26:3 shows us God's part and our part. God's part – *"Thou wilt keep him in perfect peace...."* Now, here's our part – *"...whose mind is STAYED on thee...."* It is our part to keep our minds *stayed* on God and His Word, even when circumstances, difficulties, troubling thoughts, and symptoms are trying to draw our minds in a different direction. It takes practice to keep it from going in a wrong direction when pressures come. But we can do it, or God wouldn't have told us to do it.

Over the years, when we had different dogs, we would train them to "stay" so they didn't run off after the wrong thing. You couldn't just tell them once, you had to practice with them repeatedly.

Likewise, it takes practice to keep the mind from running off, chasing wrong thoughts when they come, but if you'll keep practicing on the small, daily distractions of life, you'll be skillful at it when greater difficulties come.

This scripture reads, *"Thou wilt keep him in perfect peace, WHOSE MIND IS STAYED ON THEE...."* What does it mean to keep your mind stayed on Him? God and His Word are one. To keep your mind stayed on Him is to keep it stayed on the Word. When difficulties and circumstances come, keep your attention and your thoughts on God's Word and off of what may be opposing or surrounding you.

Let's look at the last phrase of Isaiah 26:3. *"Thou wilt keep him in perfect peace, whose mind is stayed on thee: BECAUSE HE TRUSTETH IN THEE."* To trust in God is to have faith in God.

Faith and peace are companions. You can't have one without having the other. When you're in faith, you'll be in peace, and when you're in peace, you'll be in faith. Great faith, great peace. Little faith, little peace.

We can know our faith level by looking at our peace level. If we lack peace, then we lack faith. To increase our peace, we need to increase our faith. We increase our faith by *hearing* the Word and *doing* the Word. Romans 10:17 tells us, *"So then faith cometh by hearing, and hearing by the word of God."* The more we hear the Word, the more faith comes. We can hear the Word as we feed on it and as we sit under the teaching of the Word. We then have to become a doer of the Word we heard. That's when it will make a difference in our life.

It won't do any good to pray for faith. Faith doesn't come by praying – it comes by hearing God's Word.

Our peace level reveals our faith level, or our peace level reveals the amount of faith we're releasing. Someone may *have* faith, but if they're not *releasing* it and *acting* on it, they won't be experiencing peace like they could.

The more you *do* the Word, the more the peace that's within you will rise up. So, increase your faith, but also *release* your faith by speaking and doing the Word, then you'll be in peace.

It's *faith* that compels you to keep your mind *stayed* on God and His Word when you're surrounded by difficulties, and as you do, peace will be the result – a perfect peace, an uninterrupted peace.

As you do your part, God will do His part, and perfect, uninterrupted peace will be the result and the flow of your life.

Step #4 – Think on Right Things

When we're tempted to worry, we are to stop right there and refuse to worry or be afraid. Instead we're to pray – talk to God, pour out our hearts to Him, and in faith make specific requests based on His Word. We are to then give Him thanks that He's working on our need. When we do that, God's peace will rise up and guard our hearts and minds, but we must yield to that peace that rises up.

The fourth step we're to take in casting our cares on the Lord is found in Philippians 4:8:

> **Finally, brethren, whatsoever things are TRUE, whatsoever things are HONEST, whatsoever things are JUST, whatsoever things are PURE, whatsoever things are LOVELY, whatsoever things are of GOOD REPORT; if there be any VIRTUE, and if there be any PRAISE, THINK ON THESE THINGS (fix your minds on them, AMPC).**

A thought may be true, but if it isn't lovely, refuse to think on it.

A thought must meet the criteria of all eight things listed in this verse in Philippians if we are to think on it.

The fourth step is to keep your mind set on right things – that which is true, honest, just, pure, lovely, and of good report. That's how you will maintain your peace. Refuse to let your mind return to and think on those things that were troubling you. Since you have cast those cares on the Lord, leave them there, don't take them back. Refuse to allow your mind to again touch on those things.

Second Corinthians 10:5 instructs us,

> **Casting down imaginations, and every high thing that exalteth itself against the knowledge of God** (anything that is against what God says in His Word)**, and bringing into captivity EVERY THOUGHT to the obedience of Christ.**

If a thought comes that isn't in line with God's Word and robs you of peace, you are to cast it down – refuse to turn it over in your mind.

We are to pay attention to *every* thought that comes. If a thought doesn't lead to peace, cast it down, refuse to think on it. We must obey these verses listed if we are to have a peaceful mind.

Steps To Take

Let's review the steps to casting our cares on the Lord, as we saw in Philippians 4:6-8.

When tempted to worry, or be afraid, we must refuse to. Instead we are to:

1) Pray and offer supplication – which is an earnest, heartfelt request. We are to pour out our hearts to God and make specific requests, using specific scriptures that promise us our answer and release our faith in His Word. We are placing the need in His hands.

2) Give thanks – since the need is in His hands and He is working on it, then we know the answer is ours, so in faith we give Him thanks until the answer manifests.

3) Yield to and draw on the peace within.

4) Think on right things – not allowing our minds to again think on the things that tried to trouble us or rob us of peace.

Chapter 3

Learn To Be Untroubled

God wants us to live days of Heaven on the earth. For that to happen, we must renew our mind with God's Word, which means to take on God's way of thinking. Then we must be a doer of God's Word in our everyday life.

It's not right for believers to go to church, lift their hands and praise God, then go home and live with troubled, disturbed, harassed minds.

Yes, the enemy will oppose us, and the mental arena is the enemy's greatest battleground; he's continually trying to interject wrong thinking into our thought lives. But we must learn to be untroubled and undisturbed by that opposition. We're not to wait for the devil to leave us alone (for he won't) or wait for all the circumstances of life to be perfect before we enjoy a life of peace. Rather, we must learn to live undisturbed and untroubled and be in perfect peace, no matter what the opposition or circumstances that may be surrounding or threatening us. That's victory!

Peace is not the absence of opposition; rather, it's being unmoved and undisturbed right in the face of opposition.

Peace is going to sleep and resting right in the middle of a storm and waking up without a racing, troubled mind.

Will opposition and troubling thoughts come? Undoubtedly, yes! But it's our responsibility to renew our mind with God's Word (Rom 12:1 & 2), learn who we are in Christ, learn the authority that God has given us, and exercise it. As we do God's Word and daily exercise our God-given rights and our authority over the world, the devil, and the flesh, we will live days of Heaven on this earth. As our skill with the Word grows, our level of peace grows.

Know Your Rights

To keep practicing and doing the Word in our daily lives, we must keep hearing the Word over and over. For as Romans 10:17 tells us, *"...faith cometh by hearing, and hearing by the word of God."* Through the repetition of hearing and doing the Word, we plant His Word in us and move into all God has provided for us. Repetition is how we get God's Word in us.

The devil also knows that repetition is how he can get wrong things into people, so he will repeatedly suggest or threaten something to the mind. But just because something is repeated doesn't make it true. No matter how long the devil repeats something to you – be it long or be it short – refuse to listen to it or act on it, and that strategy won't work against you.

Hosea 4:6 tells us, *"My people are destroyed for lack of knowledge...."* The word "destroyed" means cut off. God's people are "cut off" from the blessings that belong to them through the lack of knowledge, through the lack of knowing what He has provided for them, and through the lack of knowing how to exercise their victory over the devil.

Notice that the devil isn't mentioned in this verse; he's not listed as the reason God's people are destroyed or fail, for when you have knowledge of your authority over the devil and use that authority, the devil can't destroy you or cause you to fail.

As you feed on God's Word and do it, your mind becomes renewed to who you are in Christ, to what belongs to you because you belong to Christ, and to what you can do because of His power that is yours. When your mind is renewed to these truths, your life will be transformed. You will see your all-conquering authority over any enemies and opposition, including fear, worry, and doubt, and you will experience days of Heaven on the earth.

A Spiritual Giant

A spiritual giant is one whose heart and mind agree. When your thoughts and mind agree with the Word of God and agree with the faith that's in your heart (instead of arguing or reasoning against it), your spiritual life will be large. You will meet each day and each opposition as a victor, not a victim!

Wrong thoughts come to all of us, but just because they come to our minds doesn't mean they originated with our minds.

The devil's great business is to constantly try to interject wrong thinking into your thought life. But answer those thoughts. Tell him, "That's not my thought, and I won't take it," then speak God's Word to him. When you do, the devil can't accomplish his plan against you – it will fail.

The devil can't do just anything he wants to you any time he wants. If he could, why would he seek to deceive you with wrong thoughts first?

The wrong thoughts he suggests to your mind are his attempt to deceive you so he can work against you. But as you renew your mind with the Word of God (Romans 12:2), you won't be deceived, but you'll think in line and act in line with God's Word.

If your mind is continually racing, or if troubling, fearful, accusing, condemning thoughts are continually replaying over and over in your mind, that's not God. And that's not the kind of mind God authored for you.

The kind of mind God authored for us is a sound, CALM, well-balanced, disciplined, self-controlled mind (2 Tim. 1:7, AMPC).

I appreciate that the mind God authored for us is a calm mind – not a clamoring, racing, over-active, troubled, or worried mind. We must learn to quiet and calm our minds and not let them continually replay something over and over that troubles us.

Be Undisturbed

In Philippians 4:10 & 11, Paul writes to thank those who contributed to him financially while he was imprisoned for the Gospel's sake. In his letter of thanks, he makes a statement that should challenge us.

> **PHILIPPIANS 4:11 (AMPC)**
> **Not that I am implying that I was in any personal want, for I have LEARNED how to be content (satisfied to the point where I AM NOT DISTURBED OR DISQUIETED) IN WHATEVER STATE I AM.**

He wasn't saying that he was content *with* the state he was in, for he was in prison. But he was saying he had learned how to be content *in* his situation.

We're going to find ourselves in situations we're not content *with*, not wanting to stay there. But even in those times, we must learn to be content *in* those situations – being undisturbed and untroubled.

Paul was a man of great faith, and he shows us in this verse that he had to *learn* what every man of great faith must learn, *"...for I have LEARNED how to be content (satisfied to the point where I AM NOT DISTURBED OR DISQUIETED) IN WHATEVER STATE I AM."*

Practice the Word

Paul had to learn how to be undisturbed and untroubled by his circumstances. How did he learn it? The only way you learn anything – by practicing it. To become skillful at anything, whether it's natural or spiritual, you have to practice.

Take advantage of every test, trial, and difficulty to practice being a doer of the Word. That's the only way you'll become skillful with the Word and the victory that is yours.

Paul had to learn this, and so do you; you're not born knowing it.

If you'll use every minor difficulty to practice on – holding to God's Word and refusing to worry, be fearful or troubled – you will be skillful with the Word when faced with greater difficulties.

Opposition at Places of Increase

At every new phase of ministry, at every new door of greater anointing and greater revelation, there will be increased opposition. Paul tells us in 1 Corinthians 16:9, *"For a great door and effectual is opened unto me, and there are many adversaries* (at the door).*"*

Any time you come into more, there will be opposition. But if you accept the opportunities, you are also accepting the challenges. However, the challenges should not deter you from moving forward or derail you and take you off course. These challenges are to become places of practice, where you learn to do the Word and become more skillful with your victory, and where you learn to be undisturbed and untroubled by the opposition.

Peace Under Pressure

I've never been much of a worrier, even before I was saved. However, it's one thing to not be worried or troubled throughout the course of daily life, but it's a whole other thing to not be worried or troubled when the devil is attacking and opposing you. You must become skillful at living in peace and being untroubled and undisturbed when it seems that all of hell is coming against you.

This is something that Paul had learned, for he sat in that prison writing the words, *"...I have LEARNED how to be content (satisfied to the point where I am not disturbed or disquieted) in whatever state I am"* (Phil. 4:11, AMPC).

In this passage, we also see Paul's faith life demonstrated, for the life of faith is a life of peace. Although those with faith will face much opposition, the faith they possess will hold them in a place of peace, undisturbed and untroubled by what comes against them.

Faith Is Our Part

How can we have the same faith and peace that Paul experienced? We have to understand that whether or not we have strong faith is up to us, not God.

In Romans 12:3, God tells us that at the time someone is born again, He gives to them "the measure of faith;" He gives the same *beginning* measure of faith to each one of His children. But after that, it's up to that individual whether or not that measure of faith grows.

The Word is food for your faith. The more you feed on the Word and do it, the more your faith grows, for "*...faith cometh by hearing, and hearing by the word of God*" (Romans 10:17).

I get thrilled with God's Word, and I get thrilled to study or hear messages on the subject of faith. The reason it thrills me is because faith is *my* part. Power is *God's* part, but faith is *my* part. When I do *my* part and release my faith, then that opens the door for God to do *His* part and manifest His power. Faith receives God's power!

The Good Fight of Faith

At the end of Paul's life, he declared three things that summed up his life. *"I have fought a good fight, I have finished my course, I have kept the faith"* (2 Tim. 4:7). He fought a good fight and finished his course because he kept his faith – he didn't give it up, he didn't let the devil have it, he didn't let opposition and difficulties take it from him! Opposition came to get his faith, but he kept it!

You don't keep the faith without putting up a good fight, and you don't finish your course without fighting the good fight of faith!

The good fight of faith is a good fight because it's the winning fight. It's the only fight we're to engage in. Every other fight is a losing fight – the fight of worry, the fight of fear, the fight of doubt, and the fight of the mind or the emotions are all losing fights.

We're to fight the good fight – the fight of faith. We're not to even fight the devil – Jesus already defeated him. We're to fight the good fight of faith, which is to stay in faith and refuse to be swayed off God's Word.

The good fight of faith is a fight of words. When the pressures of life, difficulties, and opposition try to put wrong words in your mouth, you keep speaking God's Word and don't quit – don't give up!

Chapter 4

What's Your Attention On?

There's an important aspect of your life that affects your faith and your peace – it's your attention.

How was Paul able to be so content, undisturbed, and untroubled when he was in one of the darkest places a human can be, unjustly imprisoned? He held his attention on the right thing.

If you hold your attention on the difficulty, the opposition, and your need, it will trouble and disturb you; you'll be worried and fearful, and it will steal your faith. But if you hold your attention on God and His Word, you will be held in peace.

Your faith goes where your attention goes. If your attention is on God and His Word, that's where your faith will be; that's what you'll believe. But if your attention is on your needs, on your difficulties, and on thoughts the enemy may suggest or threaten to your mind, that's where your faith will be; that's what you'll believe.

What you put your attention on is what is drawn up into your life and gets movement in your life.

Attend to God's Words

God instructs us,

> **PROVERBS 4:20-22**
> **20 My son, ATTEND TO** (put your attention on) **MY WORDS; incline thine ear unto my sayings.**
> **21 Let them not depart from thine eyes; keep them in the midst of thine heart.**
> **22 For they are life unto those that find them, and health to all their flesh.**

God knows that our faith is affected by what our attention is on, so He tells us, *"My son, attend to* (put your attention on) *my words...."* The word "attend" means to pay attention to, to heed or listen to. We are to pay attention to and listen to what God said in His Word.

When wrong thoughts, opposition, difficulties, mental pressure, and financial pressures are trying to get our attention, God gives us a better place to look – at what He says in His Word.

God knows that the devil wants our attention, so He already told us what to do, *"...attend to MY words...."* Evidently, other words are going to want our attention – what other people may say, what circumstances say, what the reasonings of our own mind may say, and what the devil says. But God has already given us His Word and what *He* says about our situation, and we're to hold our attention there so we're not troubled by other words that come.

As we hold our attention on God's Word, we're held steady so that we stay in faith and in peace, no matter what the opposition may be, and so that we can get on the other side of tests.

Jesus As Our Example

Jesus faced great opposition, yet none of it disturbed His faith or peace. How did He do it? The Word tells us in Hebrews 12:2:

> **Looking unto Jesus the author and finisher of our faith; who FOR THE JOY THAT WAS SET BEFORE HIM ENDURED THE CROSS, despising the shame, and is set down at the right hand of the throne of God.**

This verse tells us that He was able to endure the Cross because His attention and His focus were set on the joy that awaited Him on the other side of the Cross – being seated at the right hand of the Father. His attention wasn't on the rejection, the suffering, and the shame, but His attention was on when He would be restored to His rightful place, seated next to His Father.

Not only would He be raised to that seat, but He would bring many sons to glory. We, God's children, the Body of Christ, would also be raised with Him and seated in that same seat of authority. That's what He kept His attention on, and that's how He endured.

His attention wasn't on the difficulty and the test; rather, it was on the victory. He looked clear through the Cross to the victory that was on the other side of it.

That's how we're to endure. We're to look at and put our attention on what's on the other side of the test – the victory that awaits us. We're not to allow the test to block our view of what's just on the other side of it – more promotion, more anointing, more revelation, more fruit, more increase – more!

Winning Against a Giant

When Goliath was taunting God's people and threatening their freedom, every soldier hid in fear from him, refusing to face him, because their attention was fixed on his size and the threats he made. The longer they listened to him, the more they feared him.

But when David came to the battlefield, although he saw Goliath's size and heard his threats, he didn't hide in fear. Rather, he made steps to overcome him.

Why didn't David hide in fear like the other soldiers? Because his attention wasn't on Goliath and the threats he made. His attention was on God and His ability to help him kill the giant.

David turned his attention back to the times God had helped him when he killed a lion and a bear that threatened his flocks.

But David also asked a very important question. "What's the reward for the man who kills the giant?" (1 Sam. 17:25-27).

They told him a threefold reward was offered by King Saul. He would be given great riches (immediate wealth), he would be given the king's daughter in marriage (he would marry into royalty, and his offspring would be of royal bloodline and heirs to the throne), and he and his family would be free from having to pay taxes and from serving in the military. This threefold reward wouldn't just affect him, but it would affect his whole family and all his future generations – what a reward!

All the other soldiers knew of this reward, but they still refused to fight. Why? Because their attention was so fixed on the giant that they couldn't see past him to focus on the reward. All they saw was the problem, the opposition, and they were willing to forfeit the reward.

David was a man of faith; he didn't focus on the opposition, but he focused on the God of his covenant and on what was on the other side of the opposition – the reward.

When he ran out to face Goliath, he didn't just see a giant. He saw Goliath as a big, fat bonus that would make him rich! Instead of seeing Goliath, he saw a pretty girl that would be his royal wife! When he ran to kill Goliath, he didn't see a giant. He saw a giant tax deduction for him and his whole family!

All of this would be his for just one reason – he kept his attention on God and God's greatness, rather than on Goliath and Goliath's size.

David's attention was on the right thing, and it not only affected him, but it affected his whole family and future generations.

What your attention is on doesn't always affect just you, but it can affect your whole family and future generations. When your attention is on the right things – on God, the Word, and His rewards, many are affected.

The other soldiers were fearful for one reason. Their attention was on the wrong thing. Many believers today are fearful and worried for the same reason.

Your faith goes where your attention goes. Hold your attention on God and His Word, no matter what the opposition. Then you too will be able to endure all things with joy, as you focus on and receive the reward that awaits you just on the other side of the test.

David won for one reason – he knew where to put his attention when faced with something much bigger than him.

That's what faith is – holding your attention on something greater than you and greater than the test – God and His Word.

The way to live free from fear and worry is to hold your attention on God and His Word.

Practice It

It requires practice to hold your attention on God and His Word when facing pressures, difficulties, and opposition.

But the more you practice it on the daily needs of life, the more skillful you become at it.

Live Full of the Word

In Colossians 3:16, Paul instructed us, *"Let the Word of Christ dwell in you RICHLY...."* He's telling us to live full of the Word.

When you are full of the Word, it's easier to hold your attention on God when faced with opposition. When you are less than full, it's more difficult.

As a shepherd, David spent his days in fellowship and worship of God; He held his attention on God. So when faced with Goliath, he was full – he was ready.

Live full of the Word with your attention on God, and you'll live ready.

How To Discipline Your Attention

Proverbs 4:20 & 21 instruct us, *"My son, ATTEND TO MY WORDS...."* Then the following phrases tell us how to attend to (put our attention on) His Words. *"My son, attend to my words; INCLINE THINE EAR unto my sayings. Let them not depart from THINE EYES; keep them in the MIDST OF THINE HEART."* Holding our attention on God's Word involves our ears, our eyes, and our hearts.

To hold your attention on the right thing, you will have to direct and discipline your ears, your eyes, and your heart.

Be a Good Student

In school, a student may have a good teacher and all the necessary books, but if they don't pay attention in class or study their books, they can still fail. Intelligence, good instructors, and study materials will not make up for a lack of attention.

Likewise, someone may have a Bible, be part of a wonderful local church, have the call of God on their life, and be anointed, but if they don't discipline where they allow their attention to go, they will struggle.

Incline Thine Ear

"My son, attend to my words...." The next statement tells us how to do that, *"...INCLINE THINE EAR unto my sayings* (God's Word)." *"Incline thine ear"* means to lean or bend in a particular direction. Turn your ear toward the direction of God's Word and what He says and away from what other things are saying.

Circumstances, financial needs, opposition, personal situations, people's opinions, and the reasonings of your own mind will all talk to you. You have to turn your ear away from listening to what other things are saying to you when they are in opposition to what God and His Word says.

Yes, you're going to hear other things talk to you, but that doesn't mean you have to listen to them.

You can be in your family room and have a television on and multiple family members talking all at the same time. Although all those things can be heard, you can't listen to them all at one time. You have to choose which one you are going to listen to.

Likewise, when faced with a need, you may hear many different things talking to you – circumstances, finances, opposition, etc. – but turn your ear away from them and incline your ear to God's Word; turn your ear to what He says.

You not only have to turn your natural ear toward the right direction, but also the ear of your spirit man.

What you turn your ear toward is what your attention will be on, and what your attention is on is what your faith will be on.

Fix Your Gaze

Proverbs 4:20 & 21 again reads, *"My son, attend to my words; incline thine ear unto my sayings. Let them NOT DEPART FROM THINE EYES...."* To hold your attention on God's Word and what He says, you not only have to turn your ear in His direction and to what He says in His Word, but you must also keep your eyes, your gaze, and your focus fixed on His Word.

You're going to see things opposing you in the natural arena, but that's when you have to focus the eyes of your spirit on what the natural eyes can't see. As Paul instructs us in 2 Corinthians 4:18, *"While we look not at the things which are seen (*with the natural eyes), *but at the things which are not seen (*the things of the spirit that only the eyes of faith can see): *for the things which are seen are temporal (*subject to change); *but the things which are not seen are eternal (*unchanging).*"*

When facing Calvary, Jesus kept His spiritual eyes fixed on the reward on the other side – being raised and seated at the Father's right hand and bringing many sons to glory. When David faced Goliath, he kept his spiritual eyes fixed on the God Who was far greater than the giant in front of him and on the reward that awaited him.

That's how Jesus endured. That's how David endured. That's how you will be able to endure. Don't focus on opposition that may be in full view in front of you, but with the eyes of your spirit, the eyes of faith, look past it and stay focused on what God says and shows you. What your focus is fixed on is what your attention will be on, and what your attention is on is what your faith will be on.

Keep God's Word in Your Heart

Proverbs 4:20 & 21 instructs us, *"My son, attend to my words; incline thine ear unto my sayings. Let them not depart from thine eyes, KEEP THEM* (God's words) *IN THE MIDST OF THINE HEART."* What you allow to enter your heart (your spirit) is what will govern your life, so make sure you're keeping God's Word in your heart.

Don't allow unforgiveness, bitterness, ill will, offense, pride, rebellion, fear, doubt, or any other like thing into your heart. Rather, keep the water of the Word (Eph. 5:26) flowing in freely, and all else will be washed out by the power of that cleansing Word. Live full of the Word, then there won't be room for anything else.

Our Attention Is a Channel

What we put our attention on is what will flow into our lives – good or bad.

Our attention is like a big vacuum. Whatever that vacuum passes over is what is drawn up into it. Whatever our attention passes over is what is drawn up into our lives.

Some think they have faith problems when they really have attention problems. Because they allow their attention to go to the wrong things, the wrong things are being drawn up into their lives, and then they're struggling with their faith to overcome what their attention is on. They should redirect and discipline their attention away from the wrong and troubling things and learn to hold their attention on what God says.

What the Devil Wants

One time, I saw a documentary on television about a scientist in the early 1900s who had spearheaded the development and construction of a great project. Due to living under the great pressure of his task, his mind began to break down.

One day, he told a fellow scientist, "Last night a creature came into my room and spoke to me, 'Your attention is mine, and it always will be mine!'" That man was seeing an evil spirit.

That is very revealing of what the devil is after. He didn't say, "Your life, your mind, your future, or your family are mine." No, he was after the man's attention. That demon knew that if he could get his attention, he could get everything else.

What Are You Holding On To?

One minister tells of a series of healing classes he was conducting. In order to attend, a person had to be in need of healing.

Before he started teaching, he got caught up in the Spirit and saw a vision. He saw all those present with their arms wrapped tightly around themselves, and God spoke to him, "The reason they haven't received their healing is because they're holding onto their sickness."

"What do you mean?" the minister asked. "They haven't come here to hold onto their sickness. They've come because they want to be healed."

God answered, "What they've got their minds on is what they're attending to, and what they're attending to is what they're embracing."

God was showing him that they weren't attending to God's healing Word, but they were attending to their sickness, because that's what they had their minds on.

What your mind is on is what you're attending to. What your mind is on is what your attention is on. And what your attention is on is what will gain movement in your life.

Since Jesus spoiled principalities and powers (Col. 2:15), the only power the devil has left is the power of suggestion. He will suggest troubling, fearful, worrisome, doubting thoughts to you. No person is exempt. Wrong thoughts come to everyone. But you must learn to recognize them as coming from the enemy, and resist them. Answer them with the Word of God, then tell the devil to leave. Don't entertain the thoughts he suggests by turning them over in your mind.

Those sick people who were in that healing class were still occupied with thoughts about their bodies and their symptoms instead of the Word of God they were being taught. By doing that, they were holding onto sickness instead of letting it go.

How do you let go of those wrong thoughts? By trying to get rid of them? By trying to stop them from coming? No, by answering those thoughts with God's Word, and by turning your thoughts and attention toward the Word. As you pick up God's thoughts, you end up letting go of the wrong thoughts.

Don't struggle to get rid of wrong thoughts. Speaking right words will wash out troubling thoughts.

Praising God

Also, if you will spend time praising God, it will help you to let go of wrong thoughts and turn your attention off your difficulty and onto God. Don't praise God with your need in mind, but praise God with Him and His Word, which is your answer, in mind.

Praising God will help you hold your attention on the right thing.

When tempted to be worried, fearful, or troubled, start praising God; it will turn your attention back to the right flow – God's flow.

Let Go of the Past

The people in that healing class were holding onto sickness by not letting go of their symptoms from their thought life. But you can also hold onto other things by not letting go of them out of your thought life – things like bitterness, offense, unforgiveness, hard feelings, and ill will toward others. When you hold onto those things in your thought life, you're giving them your attention, and that which gets your attention is what will gain movement in your life. Those wrong things will only grow larger and trip you up as you think about them.

If you need to, forgive others, repent of any wrongdoing, or forgive yourself, then let those thoughts of the past go out of your thought life. Instead, put your attention on the Word by being a doer of the Word.

God has authored peace for His people, but these wrong things will rob you of peace and faith. Let them go! He offers you something better and higher to hold to – His Word!

Keep Your Attention on God's Table

PSALM 23:1-5
1   **The Lord is my shepherd; I shall not want** (I will have no lack).
2   **He maketh me to lie down in green pastures** (green pastures are places of provision)**: he leadeth me beside the still waters** (Heb. – waters of quietness, not turbulent waters)**.**
3   **He restoreth my soul** (as I renew my mind with His Word, He is able to restore my soul)**: he leadeth me in the paths of righteousness for his name's sake.**
4   **Yea, though I walk through the valley of the shadow of death** (this earth, with death all around)**, I will fear no evil: for thou art with me** (as New Testament believers, He is not only "with" us, but He's now "in" us)**; thy rod and thy staff they comfort me.**
5   **THOU PREPAREST A TABLE BEFORE ME IN THE PRESENCE OF MINE ENEMIES....**

Yes, there are enemies present on this earth, but right in their presence, verse 5 tells us that something greater is also present – a table that He has prepared for us. And it's right *before* us, right in front of us. It's not behind us, it's not to the side of us, but it's right in front of us! It's in full view and within our reach! This is the table of God's Word that He has prepared and spread before all of us.

On this table is spread all the provision and blessings we will need on this earth. On the table of His Word are spread salvation, healing, prosperity, guidance, joy, peace, etc. – all the things that He has provided for His children.

Psalm 23:5 tells us that our enemies are present, but they aren't seated with us at the table. We are to quit turning our attention away from the table that God has prepared before us to put it on an enemy that Jesus has defeated. We are to quit turning our attention away from the table of God's provision, the Word, to put our attention on what a defeated enemy that is present is saying.

The enemy tries to draw us away from the table of our provision and entice our attention toward him through worry, fear, threats, suggestions, financial pressures, symptoms, relationship problems, etc.

Yes, we will hear the enemy's threats, but we don't have to listen to them. We will sense the presence of the enemy, but that doesn't mean we've failed, that our faith isn't working, or that the devil is winning. We can hear him and sense him for one reason – he is present! Don't be in awe that he's present. Don't be impressed that you may be hearing or sensing him – he is simply present.

The enemy has a right to be here on the earth because when Adam sinned, he turned his lease over to the devil.

But there will be a day when Adam's lease will run out, then Satan will be bound and cast into the bottomless pit.

You can't keep the enemy from being present, but just because he has a right to be here doesn't mean he has a right to be moving in *your* life. Don't let him gain an entrance into your life. Exercise your authority over him. Refuse to let him in.

Always approach every encounter with the enemy being mindful that he is a defeated foe, and refuse to let him into your life.

As Paul tells us in Ephesians 4:27, *"Neither give place to the devil."* The devil can't take a place in your life; you have to give him a place. But even if you've given him a place, you can it take back by being a doer of the Word and exercising your authority over him.

He has no rights over you. Once you're born again, you don't belong to him anymore! You are no longer part of his kingdom. You have been delivered from the kingdom of darkness and translated into the Kingdom of God's dear Son (Col. 1:13). Anything of the enemy's kingdom doesn't belong to you, but everything of God's Kingdom does belong to you.

Refuse to be troubled by anything of the enemy's kingdom. Refuse to listen to or be troubled by the enemy's presence. Refuse to allow anything of the enemy's thoughts and suggestions entice you or draw you away from the table of God's Word.

We must become skillful at not allowing our attention to be drawn away from the table of God's Word. Our attention and our thoughts must stay focused on what God says.

When our attention is more focused on God and what He says than on the opposition, that's when the enemy will be overcome, and we will get past that opposition. That's when we'll experience the victory that Jesus made ours.

Some Christians are so troubled, harassed, worried, and fearful because they constantly turn away from the table of the Word that's before them to listen to what the devil is saying and to see what he's doing; their attention is on him.

What your attention is on is what will gain movement in your life. So, take your attention off the devil and hold it on God's Word, no matter how the enemy tries to entice it back onto what he's doing. When you put your attention back on God's Word and what He says, you'll close the door to the enemy.

Peace in the Storm

The greatest value of God's peace isn't seen when everything is in place in your life, but when circumstances are high, when pressure can be felt, and when the storm is raging around you. Peace will cause you to be untroubled and undisturbed right in the midst of it all.

Learn to do as Jesus did when He was with His disciples in a boat that was filling up with water in a raging storm. He was so peaceful that He was able to sleep right in the midst of it (Mark 4:35-40).

Your faith in God will cause you to experience that kind of peace.

I once saw a plaque that read, "Life isn't about waiting for the storm to pass, but about learning to dance in the rain." How do you learn to dance in the rain? By learning to hold your attention on the right thing during the storm – on God's Word. Every man of great faith had to learn that.

"Oh, It's Just You!"

I love the incident told by Smith Wigglesworth, an English preacher from the early 1900s.

While sleeping one night, he was awakened by an evil presence he sensed in his room. He rolled over in his bed to see Satan sitting on the edge of his bed.

When he saw him, Wigglesworth said, "Oh, it's just you!" Then he rolled back over and went to sleep. What faith! What authority! What victory! What peace!

Some would have thought they would need to get up and engage in some kind of warfare with the devil.

Wigglesworth did deal with the devil. He answered him with a statement that expressed his complete authority over him, and he let the devil know that he wasn't impressed or awed by his presence.

Wigglesworth refused to give the devil his attention; he answered him, then just turned his back to him. That's faith! That's yielding to peace instead of to the devil!

Turn Your Back to the Enemy

As Psalm 23:5 tells us, we are seated at the table of God's provision that is spread before us. Our enemies are present, but they're not seated with us. Keep your back turned to them. That's what Jesus did in the wilderness of temptation (Luke 4). He told Satan, "Get thee behind me." That's what Wigglesworth did that night. Keep your attention off the enemy and off what he's saying and doing. That's great faith!

Those with great faith know where to look!

Some Christians have turned their attention away from the table of God's provision that's before them; they've turned their head all the way around like an owl to see what the enemy is doing all around them. Then they wonder why they struggle with their faith, don't have peace, and are so troubled.

Many are worried, fearful, depressed, have anxiety attacks and phobias (which are nothing but the spirit of fear), feel condemned, and are troubled simply because their attention is on the wrong thing.

They must learn to hold their attention on God's Word instead.

Renew Your Mind

No prayer line or ministry line will take the place of you renewing your mind with God's Word, walking in your authority, and learning to hold your attention on God's Word.

Thank God for prayer and ministry lines, but they will not do for you what only God's Word can do for you. You must hear God's Word and do it if you are to renew your mind and live a life of faith and peace. Simply hearing the Word won't renew your mind. It's when you do the Word you hear that your mind becomes renewed, and renewing your mind is something you must continue to do for the rest of your life.

The Local Church

That's why a good local church that teaches God's Word and moves with the Spirit of God is so important for you and your family. When you sit under the teaching of the Word, you have an opportunity to renew your mind with God's Word. It's the only place where you can go on a regular basis that assists you with this great work of renewing your mind.

It's only the renewed mind that will be able to enjoy a life of faith and peace and live days of Heaven on the earth.

The Simplicity of Faith

Faith is as simple as putting your attention on the right thing, on God and His Word, and turning it away from the wrong things – opposition, pressures, troubling thoughts, difficulties, needs, and surrounding circumstances.

When troubling circumstances and difficulties arise, it will require an effort on your part to hold His Word in your mouth and in your thoughts.

An Evil Spirit Overcome

Years ago, after I awoke one morning, I lay in bed and prayed in the Spirit for about 45 minutes. When I got up, I saw into the spirit realm. I saw an evil spirit crouched by my bathroom door in a pouncing position; I knew it was looking for an opportunity to gain access into my life. I also knew that I would just need to stand my ground against it.

As I got dressed, troubling thoughts bombarded my mind, but I refused to turn them over in my mind; I refused to touch them in my thought life. I answered those thoughts with God's Word, then I began to praise Him. As I praised God, it helped me to hold my attention on Him instead of on the thoughts that were coming against my mind.

I could sense the great pressure mentally, trying to draw me into the mental arena and to get me to consider the thoughts that were coming, but I refused. I refused to turn those thoughts over in my mind. The more they came, the more I praised in order to hold my attention on God.

This continued for one and a half days. I had to put forth great effort to stay my mind on God and His Word and to keep it off of the opposition and the evil presence that I sensed.

But after one and a half days of continuously staying my mind and praising God, all of a sudden that evil spirit left! I had overcome him.

Learn to discipline your attention, holding it on God and His Word, no matter what the opposition may be. Practice daily holding your attention on the right thing. As you do, you will live in victory and peace.

Chapter 5

Answer It!

An important part of faith, standing your ground on the Word, and staying in peace, is learning to answer opposition.

In Luke 4, when Jesus was in the wilderness of temptation, the devil repeatedly tempted Him. Jesus *answered* every temptation by speaking the Word of God. That was His policy of dealing with the devil. That is also to be our policy of dealing with the devil.

When the devil tempts you, threatens you, or suggests a thought to your mind, recognize that it's the devil and answer it! Don't entertain it or turn it over in your thought life, but quiet your mind and answer him from your spirit with God's Word.

When the enemy suggests or threatens you with a specific thought, answer him *specifically!* If he threatens, "You're going to lose your home," you answer him specifically in line with how he threatened you, saying, "No, I won't lose my home! For Philippians 4:19 says, *'But my God shall supply all my needs...,'* and I have a supply for my home. Now, you leave me in Jesus' Name!"

To overcome the enemy, answer specifically the threat he makes against you, then tell the spirit that spoke to you to leave, then begin to praise God. And he has to leave, for James 4:7 tells us *"...Resist the devil, and he will flee from you."*

When thoughts, pressures, and opposition try to trouble you and speak to you, don't let them have the last word, for the last word stands – answer them!

In Review

The moment circumstances, difficulties, or threatening thoughts arise, immediately:

1) Answer it specifically

2) Rebuke the spirit that spoke to you, telling it to leave

3) Praise God – for that turns your attention to God and His Word and away from the troubling thoughts and opposition

Chapter 6

Agree With God

The King James translation of Job 22:21 reads, *"Acquaint now thyself with him, and be at peace: thereby good shall come unto thee."* But I like the way the Amplified Classic Bible says it:

> **Acquaint now yourself with Him [AGREE WITH GOD and show yourself to be conformed to His will] and be at peace; by that [you shall prosper and great] good shall come to you.**

I see five things in this passage:

1) Agree with God – the more someone is acquainted with God, the more they'll agree with Him.

2) Do the Word – to "show yourself to be conformed to His will" means to be a doer of His Word. What you agree to must show up in your actions and daily life.

3) Be at peace – when you agree with God's Word and you do it in your daily life, the result will be peace. But you must yield

to that peace; don't yield to fear, worry, or doubt.

4) You will prosper – "by *that* you shall prosper." By agreeing with God and His Word and by doing it, you shall prosper.

5) Great good shall come to you – great good shall *come*. You won't have to chase it. You will be a magnet that draws all good things into every arena of your life. You will experience "great good" – spiritually, mentally, physically, financially, in your relationships, and in your family. All this will come when you agree with His Word and do it.

Worry is not agreeing with God. Fear is not agreeing with God. Doubt is not agreeing with God. Faith agrees with God; it never disagrees with Him.

It's easy to agree with God when things are going good and everything is in place. But only faith will keep agreeing with God's Word when things try to get out of place.

When symptoms come, keep agreeing with God that you're healed (Matt. 8:17, 1 Peter 2:24). When financial needs arise, keep agreeing with God that He's your Provider and shall supply all your need (Phil. 4:19). When any test or trial comes your way, don't break agreement with God's Word. Keep agreeing with God, keep doing the Word, and no matter what the pressures or circumstances are – don't quit!

That's the way to stay out of fear, doubt, and worry and stay in peace.

I listed the five things that Job 22:21 shows us. I see a divine order in that list. Notice that peace is listed third, and prosperity is listed fourth. They are preceded by the first two things – agreeing with God and doing the Word. None of these steps can be omitted. They all begin with your agreement with God and His Word.

Agree with God and do His Word despite circumstances, difficulties, and pressures; then peace, prosperity, and great good will be the result.

Chapter 7

Righteousness, Peace & Joy: A Divine Order

Romans 14:17 reads, *"For the kingdom of God is not meat and drink; but righteousness, and peace, and joy in the Holy Ghost."* Righteousness, peace, and joy is the flow God authored for us to live in while we are on the earth. We don't have to wait until we go to Heaven to enjoy this flow, for Jesus announced, *"... the kingdom of God is WITHIN you"* (Luke 17:21), and the Kingdom of God is righteousness, peace, and joy. These are within us, so they are at our disposal 24 hours a day for us to draw on.

To be in the flow of the Holy Ghost is to be moving in righteousness, peace, and joy. This is the flow in which God moves and manifests.

It's not right for a believer to not be living in peace and joy. That's the flow that belongs to us and the flow the Spirit endeavors to lead us into. Nothing else can take the place of peace and joy. Don't settle for a lesser flow.

Worry, fear, and doubt aren't God's flow; that's not the flow that belongs to us. The higher flow of God's Kingdom is what He made ours. Righteousness, peace, and joy is the flow of God's Kingdom – that's how He's flowing – so stay in that flow to stay in the flow of the Spirit of God.

A Divine Order

When I read Romans 14:17, I see a divine order there. *"The kingdom of God is...righteousness, and peace, and joy...."*

1) Righteousness

2) Peace

3) Joy

Romans 5:17 tells us that righteousness is having right standing with God, being right with God. Jesus has made you righteous (1 Cor. 1:30). His righteousness is your righteousness. You're not righteous because *you've* done everything right. You're righteous because *Jesus* did everything right.

When you were born again, you were made righteous. You are no longer to live under the consciousness of the sin, guilt, and shame of your past. The Blood of Jesus cleansed you of all of that at the new birth, when you were born again.

Once you're born again, if you do miss God and sin, then repent, confess that to God, and He will cleanse you; then you are again righteous. For 1 John 1:9 reads, *"If we confess our sins, he is faithful and just to forgive us our sins, and to cleanse us from all unrighteousness."*

Because you are righteous, you should no longer live conscious of past sins, faults, or failures. It pleases God when you believe that by Jesus' Blood you have been cleansed and forgiven. When God forgives, He forgets. Once you repent, forgive yourself and forget it too. For if you don't, you won't live as one who has been made righteous.

One of the greatest actions of faith you can make is to again stand back up in your righteousness, living as though you never missed it, once you have confessed it to God and received by faith the cleansing of the Blood. That's how you keep the door closed to condemnation, sin-consciousness, guilt, and shame.

Guilt, condemnation, and shame will cause you to draw back from living as one who has been made righteous. You won't exercise your authority over the devil as you should or take advantage of the rights and privileges that are yours in Christ.

Agree with God that He has made you righteous, and live that way. That pleases Him, for that's faith.

When you are living in your righteousness, you will walk in your authority over the devil, the world, and the flesh. You will walk in the rights and privileges that are yours because you are in Christ. You won't allow any of those things or your past to hold you back from walking with God and from exercising your rights and privileges in Christ.

When you're walking in your righteousness, you will stand against the enemy when he opposes you; you will exercise your authority over him. When you take your authority over the devil, refusing to let him work in your life, then you will walk in victory, and you'll have peace and joy in your life.

Peace & Joy

Remember the divine order we see in Romans 14:17 – righteousness, peace, and joy. Righteousness precedes peace. If you're to have peace, you must first walk in your righteousness, which includes taking your authority over the devil when he opposes you. Refuse to live under the guilt, condemnation, or shame of your past.

If you're walking in your righteousness, when fear, doubt, or worry comes, you exercise your authority over them; you refuse to yield to them. If you'll stand against them, you'll have peace.

In the divine order we see in Romans 14:17, there's righteousness, peace, and joy. As I said, you must walk in your righteousness if you're to live in peace. But you must also walk in peace if you're to experience joy.

Believers who are fearful, doubting, and worried will forfeit their peace, but they will also forfeit their joy.

No one can live a life of joy if they're not living in peace.

Yield to Peace & Joy

The peace and joy that belong to us as believers is not a natural peace or joy that flows from outward circumstances.

Rather, the peace and joy that belong to us are spiritual forces that God has made ours, and they flow independent of circumstances; they are not dependent upon the circumstances of our lives being peaceful and joyful.

Peace and joy are two of the nine fruits of the spirit that are already in your spirit. They are in you; they were made yours at the new birth. Because they are in your spirit, they are at your disposal 24 hours a day. As you yield to them, they will flow.

When troubling circumstances, pressures, or difficulties arise, you can draw on the peace and joy that are in you and yield to them instead of to what is coming against you.

You yield to peace and joy and draw them up out of your spirit by praising and rejoicing.

Learn to praise, rejoice, and laugh when faced with difficulties. You're not rejoicing or laughing because you're facing difficulties; rather, you're rejoicing and laughing because that's how you dip down into your spirit and draw up the peace and joy that is within you.

God put those spiritual forces of peace and joy in your spirit so you can draw them out anytime you need them.

You don't have to wait for God or the anointing to come on you. You don't have to wait for the preacher to pray for you. You can choose to draw them out anytime you want to. You don't have to wait for a crisis or difficulty to come before you draw them out. You can draw on them every day! Righteousness, peace, and joy are to be the flow of your daily life.

Practice drawing them up from your spirit every day, even when you're not facing difficulties; then you'll already be skillful at doing it when difficulties arise.

When worry, difficulties, or fear come, instead of yielding to them and opening the door to them, draw out peace and joy. And when you do, those difficulties, worries, and fears that you face can't get an open door into your life, and they will be overcome and fall away.

The circumstances of life won't always offer you peace and joy, but that's not a problem – you brought your own! Peace and joy are already IN you – so draw them out right in the face of difficult or troubling circumstances.

Circumstances aren't the source of your peace and joy anyway – GOD IS!

In Conclusion

Righteousness, peace, and joy are yours. They are the flow of God's Kingdom, and they are the flow of the Holy Ghost, the flow He endeavors to lead us into. It's the flow God gets involved in.

As you operate in the righteousness, peace, and joy that God has made yours, you will live the life that God authored for you to live – days free from worry, fear, and doubt – days of Heaven on the earth!

Prayer of Salvation

Heavenly Father, I come to You in the Name of Jesus. Your Word says, *"...him that cometh to me I will in no wise cast out"* (John 6:37). So I know You won't cast me out, but You will take me in, and I thank You for it.

You said in Your Word, *"...If thou shalt confess with thy mouth the Lord Jesus, and shalt believe in thine heart that God hath raised him from the dead, thou shalt be saved. For whosoever shall call upon the name of the Lord shall be saved"* (Rom. 10:9 & 13).

I believe in my heart that Jesus Christ is the Son of God. I believe Jesus died for my sins and was raised from the dead so I can be in right-standing with God. I am calling upon His Name, the Name of Jesus, so I know, Father, that You save me now.

Your Word says, *"...with the heart man believeth unto righteousness; and with the mouth confession is made unto salvation"* (Rom. 10:10). I do believe with my heart, and I confess Jesus now as my Lord. Therefore, I am saved! Thank You, Father.

Please write us and let us know that you have just been born again.
When you write, ask to receive our salvation booklets.

To contact us, please email us at
dm@dufresneministries.org
or write to:
Dufresne Ministries
P.O. Box 1010
Murrieta, CA 92564

How To Be Filled With the Holy Spirit

Acts 2:38 reads, *"...Repent, and be baptized every one of you in the name of Jesus Christ for the remission of sins, and ye shall receive the GIFT of the Holy Ghost."* The Holy Ghost is a gift that belongs to each one of God's people. Jesus is the gift God gave the whole world, but the Holy Spirit is a gift that belongs only to God's people.

Jesus told His disciples, *"But ye shall receive POWER, after that the Holy Ghost is come upon you: and ye shall be witnesses unto me..."* (Acts 1:8). When you're baptized with the Holy Spirit, you receive supernatural power that enables you to live victoriously.

Indwelling vs. Infilling

When you're born again, you receive the indwelling of the Person of the Holy Spirit. Romans 8:16 tells us, *"The Spirit itself* (Himself) *beareth witness with our spirit, that we are the children of God."* When you're born again, you know it because the Spirit bears witness with your spirit that you are a child of God; He confirms it to you. He's able to bear witness with your spirit because He's in you; you are *indwelt* by the Spirit of God.

But the Word of God speaks of another experience subsequent to the new birth that belongs to every believer, and that is to be baptized with the Holy Spirit, or to receive the *infilling* of the Holy Spirit.

God wants you to be full and overflowing with the Spirit. Being filled with the Spirit is likened to being full of water. Just because you had one drink of water doesn't mean you're full of water. At the new birth, you received the indwelling of the Spirit – a drink of water. But now God wants you to be filled to overflowing – be filled with His Spirit, baptized with the Holy Ghost.

> **ACTS 2:1-4**
> **1 And when the day of Pentecost was fully come, they were all with one accord in one place.**
> **2 And suddenly there came a sound from heaven as of a rushing mighty wind, and it filled all the house where they were sitting.**
> **3 And there appeared unto them cloven tongues like as of fire, and it sat upon each of them.**
> **4 And they were all FILLED with the Holy Ghost, and BEGAN TO SPEAK WITH OTHER TONGUES, as the Spirit gave them utterance.**

When these disciples were filled with the Holy Ghost, they began to speak with other tongues as the Spirit gave them utterance; they spoke in a language unknown to them. Today, when a believer is filled with the Holy Ghost, they will speak with other tongues too. These are not words that come from the mind of man, but they are words given by the Holy Spirit; these words float up from their spirit within, and the person then speaks those out.

What is the benefit of being filled with the Holy Ghost with the evidence of speaking in other tongues? First Corinthians 14:2 reads, *"For he that speaketh in an unknown tongue speaketh not unto men, but unto God...."* When you're speaking in other tongues, you're speaking to God – it is a divine means of communicating with your Heavenly Father. This is one of many great benefits.

> **MATTHEW 7:7-11**
> **7 Ask, and it shall be given you...**
> **8 FOR EVERY ONE THAT ASKETH RECEIVETH...**
> **9 ...what man is there of you, whom if his son ask bread, will he give him a stone?**
> **10 Or if he ask a fish, will he give him a serpent?**
> **11 If ye then, being evil, know how to give good gifts unto your children, HOW MUCH MORE SHALL YOUR FATHER WHICH IS IN HEAVEN GIVE GOOD THINGS TO THEM THAT ASK HIM?**

In this passage, Jesus is saying that when you ask God for something, you shall receive it! Believe that He will give you that which you ask for. When you ask God for something good, He won't give you something that will harm you; He will give you the good thing you ask for. The baptism of the Holy Spirit is a good gift, and when you ask God to fill you with the Holy Spirit, you won't receive a wrong spirit; you will receive this good gift, the gift of the Holy Spirit.

Once you receive the gift of the Holy Ghost, you can yield to this gift any time, speaking in other tongues as often as you choose; you don't have to wait for God to move on you. The more you speak in other tongues, the more you will benefit from this gift. By continuing to speak in other tongues on a daily basis, you will be able to maintain a Spirit-filled life; you will live full of the Spirit.

The more you take time to speak in other tongues, the deeper you'll move into the things of God.

(For more teaching on being filled with the Holy Spirit, I recommend the mini-book, *Why Tongues?* by Kenneth E. Hagin.)

Prayer To Receive the Holy Spirit

"Father, I see that the gift of the Holy Spirit belongs to Your children. So, I come to You to receive this gift. I received my salvation by faith, so I receive the gift of the Holy Spirit by faith. I believe I receive the Holy Spirit now! Since I'm filled with the Holy Spirit now, I expect to speak in other tongues as the Spirit gives me utterance, just like those in Acts 2 on the Day of Pentecost. Thank You for filling me with the Holy Ghost."

Now, words that the Spirit of God gives you will float up from your spirit. You are the one who must open your mouth and speak those words out. The words will not come to your mind, but they will float up from your spirit. Speak those out freely.